LOVE UPSIDE DOWN

You'll be disappointed in Love Upside Down if you expect to find something you missed in the Kama Sutra! Steven Ogden's starting point is a late Iron Age activist named Jesus, a subversive who "caused great scandal in the name of love". Engaging, reflective and challenging.
David Boulton, author, *The Trouble with God* and *Who on Earth was Jesus?*

In Love Upside Down: Life, Love and the Subversive Jesus, Steven G. Ogden stirs up amidst the messiness of life the "exquisite moments of love" that change us – our perceptions and our behaviors. And as we are turned upside down, we acquire "new eyes" with which to take others seriously. Ogden gets very personal: we not only change our regard for ourselves, but also acquire the kind of love that can change the world. As he shows – even if love cannot "cure all that ails...it can help us live with dignity and hope."
James A Kowalski, Dean, The Cathedral Church of St John the Divine, New York.

Love is one of the most abused words in contemporary language. And yet love lies at the heart of religious faith, and is at the very center of what it means to understand and practice the presence of God, and live life after the example of Jesus. In this profound, wise and probing book, Steven Ogden opens up new vistas on the meanings of love for the shaping of our faith. Alternately challenging and comforting, we are brought face to face with the simple yet radical message of the gospel. This is a stimulating and refreshing book that will inspire all who those seek to deepen their discipleship in today's world.
Martyn Percy, Principal, Ripon College Cuddesdon and The Oxford Ministry Course

In the tradition of Richard Holloway's Doubts and Loves, Steven Ogden has written a heart-searching exploration of the Christian understanding of what it means to love. In the process he has re-evaluated how we love as Christians; and what that is in relation to living in postmodernity. Ogden has desanitized Jesus; and got down and dirty in the real world. He has not flinched from tackling the serious theological and ethical issues that confront Christians today. This is honest, raw theology which is unfortunately eschewed by so many academics and Christian writers. This book is not only confronting but uplifting as well. My advice – read it!

Nigel Leaves, author, *The God Problem* former Warden Wollaston Theological College, Western Australia

What is love? At its heart is a wondering seeing of another person – seeing them in their full reality, as if for the very first time. To see in this way is impossible unless we are willing to be vulnerable, above all to be vulnerable to the otherness of the Other. And to be this vulnerable is impossible unless we have learned in some measure to love and accept ourselves. So Steven Ogden shows the inner logic of Jesus' commandment that we love one another as we love ourselves. In this accessible and daring book, Steven Ogden shows how the quirky kingdom preached by Jesus can change our world with the power of love, and challenges the church to live as if it really is the foretaste of that new reality.

Sarah Bachelard, Lecturer in Theology, St Mark's National Theological Centre, Charles Sturt University

Love
Upside Down

Life, Love and the
Subversive Jesus

Love
Upside Down

Life, Love and the
Subversive Jesus

Steven Ogden

BOOKS

Winchester, UK
Washington, USA

First published by O-Books, 2011
O-Books is an imprint of John Hunt Publishing Ltd., Laurel House, Station Approach,
Alresford, Hants, SO24 9JH, UK
office1@o-books.net
www.o-books.com

For distributor details and how to order please visit the 'Ordering' section on our website.

Text copyright: Steven Ogden 2010

ISBN: 978 1 84694 546 5

All rights reserved. Except for brief quotations in critical articles or reviews, no part of
this book may be reproduced in any manner without prior written permission from
the publishers.

The rights of Steven Ogden as author have been asserted in accordance with the Copyright,
Designs and Patents Act 1988.

A CIP catalogue record for this book is available from the British Library.

Design: Stuart Davies

Printed in the UK by CPI Antony Rowe
Printed in the USA by Offset Paperback Mfrs, Inc

We operate a distinctive and ethical publishing philosophy in all
areas of our business, from our global network of authors to
production and worldwide distribution.

CONTENTS

ACKNOWLEDGMENTS

I am grateful for the interest and support of Norm Hunter, Nigel Leaves, Gloria Parker, Lee Parker, Susan Crothers-Robertson and Hannah Robertson. They all played their part in the evolution of this work of love.

Our sons Lachlan, Duncan and Sam, have taken an active interest in the project. Their spontaneity and clarity have always been welcome.

Anne my wife, friend and lover, has taught me much about love, perhaps the hardest lessons of all. Her presence and courage permeate this book.

Steven Ogden

PREFACE

Oh no, not another book on love? But this is different. This is for people who are looking for a gritty account of life, love and the quandaries of human existence. It is written for those who want an authentic account of love that respects human experience, but which is able to mine the depths of a greater wisdom.

I tap into the Christian tradition, but there is no old man in the sky pulling the strings. There is no bible bashing here. This is an exploration for 21st century thinkers and lovers. It is designed for all sorts of people, from searching Christians to broad minded agnostics and atheists, who are interested in love.

As I look back on my life, it is the exquisite moments of love that have given me the elation of grace and the consolation of dignity. This is because love puts everything in perspective; it forms a new horizon that enables me to say "This doesn't matter" or "This matters and I will risk everything".

The cutting edge for this horizon of love comes from my experience of re-visiting Christianity. On my return, I discovered not the meek and mild Jesus of Sunday school fame; but the subversive Jesus of the first century, who caused great scandal in the name of love. The problem with Jesus is that for him: people were more important than venerable institutions, governing principles and religious dogma.

For many of us, this is not the kind of love we expected. This is love upside down. But there is no *hocus pocus*, it is about changing our perceptions and how that changes who we are. Its key characteristic is how we see others. When we begin to see others, when we take them seriously, we see them for the first time.

A DIFFERENT KIND OF SEEING

This is an invitation to explore and celebrate love, but by love I am not talking about the bloodless love of television sitcoms, romance novels and glossy magazines. On the contrary, I am talking about the love that we have lost and found, agonized over and delighted in. This love is grounded in our experience, and while we have not figured it out, we are still fascinated. This love is big-hearted, fearless and generous to a fault.

While love will not solve all the problems faced by humankind, it can make us fully human and create more humane communities. The key to understanding this love is how we see other people; but it is a different kind of seeing that changes who we are. So, let's begin this exploration with a tale of young love.

Love at First Sight

The evening was made for love. The planets were aligned and the sky was clear, with a full moon set among a dazzling array of stars. A throng of teenage boys made their way to the girls' cabin, with the stealth of a finely tuned commando unit. There was no turning back.

The summer holiday camp took place in low-lying mountains on the outskirts of the city. The teachers, who were responsible for the well-being of a hundred thirteen year olds, were sound asleep. We knew this because we had carefully studied their movements over the last three days.

Trevor, the captain of the school football team, tapped nervously on the door of the girls' cabin. His diffidence was uncharacteristic. Nevertheless, it was a barometer of the weight of expectation. Immediately Rachel, the school's chess champion, opened the door and squealed with delight. We poured in. The cabin, consisting of 4 double bunks, was brimming with 16 giggling adolescents. The mind boggles.

As I made my way into the middle of the cabin, I looked up and saw Sally sitting on top of her bunk, quietly surveying the scene below. She was diminutive, with blue eyes and a beautiful radiant-smile. I liked Sally a great deal. I had spoken to her at school on a few occasions with some stunning remarks like "May I borrow your red pen?" or "What did the teacher say?" These gems were excuses to establish a connection. With every exchange, she spoke with warmth and grace beyond her years. The fact I was not one of the in-group only accentuated the deep and enduring impression she made on me.

Earlier that day, Trevor, Rachel and Sally decided in advance that we would play spin the bottle. This was an ancient pastime, probably invented by courtesans in the middle Ages, which now provided teenagers with ample opportunity for kissing. It was a simple game. To begin, a bottle was placed in the center of the room, with the girls and boys forming a circle around the bottle. Then everyone present would take turns to spin the bottle. When the bottle stopped spinning, the bottle spinner had to kiss the boy or girl directly opposite this glass pointer. It was pure genius.

It was my turn. I picked up the bottle, which weighed heavily in my shaking hand. I looked up and yes, Sally was smiling at me with *that* radiant smile. With determination, I gave the bottle an almighty spin and as a consequence it took forever to stop. When it did, it was pointing at Sally. The cabin was silent. I inched forward with my heart beating uncontrollably. As I motioned to kiss Sally, I noticed her beautifully shaped crimson mouth was slightly open. Without thinking, I closed my eyes at the point of consummation, but instead of the anticipated bliss, there was an eruption of wild laughter and barefaced scorn. I opened my eyes to find Sally pulling away and scurrying back up into the safety of her bunk. I was mortified.

I turned around and moved slowly staring at the cabin floor and then I slumped corpse-like on a bottom level bunk. It was a small death. I would have gladly gone to the grave then and there. It was partly out of embarrassment, but it was more out of a sense of loss. Soon realizing that I looked ridiculous, I sat up quickly and pretended to be jolly. The group had long forgotten my demise and was now concentrating on the next spin of the bottle. Instinctively, I cast an eye at Sally, only to find she was looking at me. She looked a little teary, which only made her more beautiful. Curiously, she was not staring. She was not coy. She was simply looking at me, as if to say "this is a little crazy, but I care". At that precise moment, I fell in love.

I had seen Sally many times before. I knew what she looked like. I knew her friends. I knew some of her interests. But I saw her differently now. It was as though I saw Sally for the first time. In that sense, it was love at first sight, but it was a different kind of seeing. This was a mutual apprehension of the other, a dawning and a recognition that created a bond between us. Once she was a girl at school, but now she was Sally. Yes, even her name took on new meaning. For a moment, there was a spark of love.

Love is personal, but it is not small or trivial. It is our link with the world. Love is complex. It is hard to define. It is subject to change yet capable of longevity, through thick and thin, success and failure, triumph and tragedy. From Shakespeare and Jane Austen to *Seinfeld* and *Fawlty Towers*: love is tragic, tragicomic and just plain comic. Yet it is redeeming, even transcendent. And all this was true of my encounter with Sally. For many reasons my relationship with Sally soon faded away. But even now, her name calls to mind an experience of love.

When Sally looked at me that night, with such sweet tenderness, her very being evoked something decent and wonderful from within me. I had not expected this at all. Naturally, this brief encounter included her smiling face, her demur manner and feisty spirit, but there was something about her as a whole person, which was a source of surprise and wonder. For a moment, an exquisite moment, my horizons, my perception and my world had changed.

Where Am I Going and Why

I am exploring love and how love changes our perceptions and behavior. In particular love, by changing us, dramatically changes the way we relate to other people, because it helps us deal with the problem of difference. Differences, like gender, can be threatening making people feel vulnerable and do irrational and destructive things. From a Christian perspective, love is a force to be reckoned with, because it turns us upside down. It does this by drawing us into the life of love, such that we gladly embrace those who are different. But it is profoundly counter-cultural.

I will develop these themes later, but it is important to signal them now. In Chapter 2, I will explore what I am calling *love-substitutes* and their relationship to vulnerability. Love-substitutes are cheap imitations of the real thing. I will concentrate, however, on why human beings feel vulnerable in the face of difference, where difference covers things like gender or sexuality. In chapter 3, I will develop the theme of the horizon of love. The horizon of love is the big picture that puts the details of our lives into perspective. I also will name Christianity's unwanted baggage and focus on Jesus and his passionate commitment to love. This is a pivotal chapter because it brings together several themes and spells out my perspective on love, which provides the foundation for the next three chapters. The key is once we see other people differently, we act differently and we are transformed in the process. In chapters 4, 5 and 6, I will look at the impact of love in relation to women, ecology and homosexuality. The important question is: why do some people react negatively toward women, the environment and lesbian and gay people? I will also use the chapter on homosexuality as an opportunity to draw together and develop further the themes of vulnerability, difference and the power of love to renew people and communities. In chapter 7, I will outline the future possibilities of love and the ways it can turn our world upside down. Lastly, I am writing largely for a Western context that includes Europe, North America, Australia and New Zealand.

My primary concern is to develop a general approach to the complex matters we face in the 21st century. So I want to invite you to join with me in an exploration and celebration of love, on the basis that love can provide a creative, compassionate and just response to complex matters. Throughout, I am celebrating a particular understanding of love, which invites us to take others seriously. This means we pause to gaze at the other person and maybe, just maybe, we see and understand them for the first time. In the process we are re-born, as there is something about the other person that draws out the best in us. I am calling this approach *the horizon of love*.

In my case, the cutting edge for the horizon of love comes from re-visiting Christianity. This presumes two things: there are parts of the Christian tradition we need to let go, but there are other aspects that are remarkable, in particular its approach to love as expressed in the life of Jesus. Every time I re-visit Christianity, this becomes more apparent. Specifically, the impact of the experience of re-visiting the figure of Jesus has made a profound impression on the way I see the world. I have new eyes. Jesus is no longer meek and mild, but a passionate, wisdom teacher of love.

The teachings of Jesus focused on *the kingdom of God*. This theme is of great importance in the development of the horizon of love. The Greek word, which we translate as kingdom, is *basileia*. It relates to the active presence of God in the world, both now and in the future. In contrast, the English word *kingdom* has tangible associations ranging from kings, queens, courtly behavior and venerable institutions, to visiting Buckingham Palace. The contemporary associations are conventional and static in nature. In contrast, the kingdom of God is intangible, unconventional and dynamic. It is a quirky, subversive and non-violent kingdom, turning the world upside down; turning it up the right way. While it is not a physical entity, it has practical outcomes. Above all, the kingdom of God is characterized by an indefinable generosity of spirit and an excess of grace that begins and ends in love. And yes, love is enough, it is more than enough.

For convenience sake, I will use the English word *kingdom*. But I will mix it up, in order to show the richness of the concept. Among others, I will also use *the quirky kingdom* or *the reign of God*. Intriguingly, Jesus often uses the metaphor of *the banquet* to describe the kingdom of God. This is an inclusive banquet, which breaks the social convention of allocating the seats of honor to the elite members of society. So *the quirky banquet* also captures the spirit of *the kingdom of God*. In the end, however, you cannot pin down the kingdom of God and this is partly why Jesus described it in parables.

So, I am celebrating the theme of love. In Christianity, love is the decisive and defining value of all things *Christian*, but it is subversive; this is love upside down. Such love is not for the fainthearted, because it changes who we are and the world we live in. One of its key characteristics relates to the way we see others, because love begins when we look at others as irreplaceable. When we begin to see others, we see them for the first time. Recall the game of spin the bottle? I had seen Sally many times, but suddenly I saw her differently or rather, it was a different kind of seeing. Once we see people this way, then the other characteristics of love emerge and flourish. Such love is

6

courageous, big-hearted and inclusive. We accept people. We invite them into our lives as they are. Significantly, they bring out the best in us.

The Love Horizon

I am interested in how love changes the regard we have for ourselves, other people and the world. Such love involves a different kind of seeing. Yes, it is a way of apprehending people, so that we see them for the first time. In a real way, it can be love at first sight. So, love has the capacity to provide a broad horizon for living and loving. In particular, love has the capacity to open up new horizons. The German philosopher Hans-Georg Gadamer put it this way: "The horizon is the range of vision that includes everything that can be seen from a particular vantage point. Applying this to the thinking mind, we speak of narrowness of horizon, of the possible expansion of horizon, of the opening up of new horizons... ".

This is important because we do not live in a vacuum. At least implicitly, we live and make life choices with a background or framework in mind. This is our horizon. To put it another way, sometimes we develop a greater appreciation of what is going on in the foreground, by means of a renewed appreciation of the background. With a limited horizon, there is a danger that we will remain captive to a limited vision of others and the world; that is we cannot see the wood for the trees. A new or expanded horizon gives us a new angle, a wider perspective, and the sense that there is more *out there* than we can ever comprehend. It opens up our thinking, so that we are able to canvas other ways of seeing and living. This can provide us with a sense of purpose and a *feel* for our place in the world. An expanded horizon also fosters a degree of modesty about what we can claim in terms of our own values and beliefs.

I am making a claim for the inclusion of love on the horizon of our living, thinking and decision making. When love is the horizon, or our horizon is expanded to include love, we look at others with new eyes. For love, as the horizon, changes the way we see people. As in art, if we change a painting's frame, then the painting is changed because we see the painting differently.

Love, by transforming our perceptions, makes it possible to change the way we see and live. All this rests on three assumptions. First, our response to others is related to how we see them. How we see them is related to a host of things like family of origin, culture, personal experience and present circumstance as well as the horizon in which these things are played out. Second, love as an emotion is not just an irrational response, springing up from nowhere; on the contrary, it is intimately related to our deepest thoughts, value judgments and intentions. Third, love has ethical implications. So while I am not writing a book on ethics, love changes the way we approach ethical dilemmas by changing the way we see the people involved. So, let us digress for a moment just to appreciate the ethical implications of love.

Ethical Implications

The horizon of love shapes and colors the way we approach life and in particular, the way we approach ethical decisions. I am not, however, writing an ethics book (a specialist area in its own right) let alone a dry and dusty academic tome. I am focusing on life, that is lived human experience, and inviting you to join me in exploring experience in the light of love.

For a moment, the focus is on ethics and the horizons of ethical decision making. The importance of this context is highlighted by the fact that the field of ethics cannot be reduced to a rule book or a road map. It is not that simple. There is no clear consensus about how to resolve moral dilemmas or define concepts like ethics and morals. The only clear agreement is that ethical issues are complex. In addition, many of us have endured professional workshops on ethics, where an eloquent speaker with polished power-point presentation and lively group discussions, takes us back to people like Aristotle, only to conclude that there is no conclusion. As a result, the boss ticks the risk management box and gets us to sign-off on a professional code of ethics, thus covering the managerial backside. But we need to move beyond mere theory.

The complexity of moral dilemmas demands sensitivity. There is a lot at stake. Namely, people make moral decisions, but often other people pay the price for the consequences of those decisions. They have to wear it. So, rather than attempting to solve these dilemmas, we need to be clear about what we bring to them. How do we look at the issues? How do we see the people involved? Within which particular horizon, do we do our looking and seeing?

Life is messy. The complexity of the mess, however, does not mean we abandon ethical concern. It means that the concern needs to be taken seriously and this involves taking people seriously. If there is one thing that I have learned from re-visiting Christianity, then it is the priority of real people over abstract principles. At the least, start with people and then adapt and apply the principles. As the Australian philosopher Raimond Gaita argues, ethical reflection involves a personal response to people in real dilemmas:

> The fact that there can be no manual of morals, no theory of its practice which plays the same role as does mountaineering theory to mountaineering practice, no quiz shows or no whizz kids of moral dilemmas and no Nobel Laureates in Morality, is intrinsic to our understanding of what it is to have a moral problem and what it is to think about it. We often express this by saying that moral problems are personal.

This means making moral decisions is hard work, because they are *our* decisions. We cannot blithely defer the responsibility for making these decisions to someone else, without diminishing the integrity of our own moral core. It is no good simply bleating that a philosopher or a theologian, a priest or a pastor has said "You must believe this" or "You should do that". If we do, we fail ourselves as well the people who are caught up in the dilemma. In fact, as we approach an ethical dilemma in the real world, we would do well to begin by setting aside our *principles* and focusing on *people*. In other words, we should, at the least temporarily, refrain from making abstract judgments about concrete situations. Maybe then, and only then, are we in position to see what practical wisdom can be gleaned from the situation.

We make moral decisions in response to others at a certain time, in a certain place, in the face of a specific dilemma. In particular, for Gaita there is an important link between resolving a particular dilemma and how we see the people involved. This is a significant insight and I want to build on this. But I want to go one step further. In Christianity, we are explicitly called to see people from within the horizon of love and in turn this love changes us and the way we see others. Remember, with Sally it was love at first sight, but it was a different kind of seeing. So, when it comes to ethical issues, the challenge is to see the people concerned *as people*. This means that there is an important shift from cool detachment to real engagement, such that the people concerned are not objects under a microscope, but partners in a conversation.

Leaving the Nest

My exploration of the theme of love involves revisiting Christianity in order to see what it says about love. Christianity, however, has a lot of baggage. Some of it needs to be addressed and ejected, but there is some good stuff too. It is the good stuff that has inspired and stretched me. This is what I want to explore.

At some stage, people need to leave the Church, at least emotionally, burning bridges and kicking the traces. If we do not leave, then we do not become our own persons. In other words, we have to leave in order to develop a deeper understanding and appreciation of faith. Call it a desert experience. It is the great paradox: a loss of faith, or a period of un-faith, is often the forerunner of a deeper faith. Certainly, the new experience and understanding of faith will have some of the old elements, but we will be different. Hopefully, this new faith will be expressed in the life of a passionate faith community, but it does not become *ours* unless and until we cut the ecclesial umbilical cord. Let me explain.

I am not trying to empty churches. On the contrary, this is a plea for a deeper, more mature, more reasonable spiritual life. The reality is that the Church, for good or ill, is like a mega-parent figure. Look at the language (Holy Father, Mother Church). Unintentionally, in some cases intentionally, there is always the risk of the Church fostering an unhealthy codependence between itself and its people. It is part of the downside of large, hierarchical institutions. But psychologically and spiritually, we have to separate. We need to leave the nest. In many instances, however, people do not have to leave the Church physically to develop a mature understanding of faith. But there has to be a significant level of disengagement, so that we can return afresh and reclaim a sense of faith in a new way. In terms of the risk of codependence, there are some advantages in not being raised in the Church. Arguably, there is less baggage and we also avoid the risk of being inoculated against faith in early life by a second rate or bloodless Christianity. Nonetheless, many Christians have been raised in faith communities that have given them the permission and encouragement to take risks and develop an independent and courageous sense of faith.

All this is part of the psychological and spiritual work of developing an adult understanding of faith. We are no longer small children, living under the watchful eye of an old man with a long beard on a throne in the sky. As children, we felt protected by God, families, school teachers, kindly nuns as well as Father

Christmas, the Easter Bunny and the Tooth Fairy. Much of this was apt for the psychological and spiritual capacities of a child. But we aren't children anymore.

I work on the premise, and out of the experience, that the spiritual journey is not just a pleasant walk in a park with birds singing and flowers blooming. Invariably, there are major disruptions along the way. Typically, these tectonic events occur in the period immediately after a personal crisis, when we begin to question ourselves, our beliefs and our relationships. The *wilderness* phase is a period in which we outgrow older ways of seeing, believing and relating. This involves an element of grief, but this is a precursor to a new and exciting period of understanding and integration.

I left the Church in my adolescence. This was partly about me coming to terms with my family of origin, but it was also because I found the experience of church meaningless. Yet, at the time of leaving, I recall a sense of wistfulness for what I had lost, because my childhood faith provided an indefinable sense of comfort and security. I had felt safe in the womb. I returned to the Church in my 20s with a sense of exhilaration, but it was not the same faith as my childhood.

I have remained in the Church ever since, but I am not entirely captive to the institution. I love the life of faith in community with other travelers. I regard the Church with affection and gratitude, but I try to maintain a sense of ambivalence toward it as an institution. What's more, a robust faith that incorporates doubt is a life-long process of leaving and returning. So, while I have not physically left the Church since my adolescence, I have had significant phases of disengagement. At times, I have wisely withdrawn to a figurative or psychological desert. I used to beat up on myself for this, but now I see it as life giving. It is part of the spiritual journey. And every time I return, I fall in love again for the very first time.

Response to Others

Does all this sound too good to be true? Or worse still, is this another self-help book? Let me be clear, this is not a crafty version of the power of positive thinking. This is no starry-eyed ode to love, glossing over the fractured nature of human existence. We have had enough of celluloid fantasies, with perfect teeth and happy endings, parading utopian visions of the life we are supposed to be living. No, I am interested in love in real life.

In reality, we know that love alone will not fix everything. Group hugs will not always advance the cause of humankind. At the macro level, there are immense social and political problems in the world. At the micro level, there are annoying people. Life is complex. As the novelist Nabokov said, "Existence is a series of footnotes to a vast, obscure, unfinished masterpiece". So let's start talking about love as we find it in the world. *Real* love is a complex thing; wonderful and exasperating, humanizing but elusive. Nonetheless, while love may not cure baldness, remove world poverty or solve world peace, it can change people, communities and cultures. Love does not cure all that ails, but it can help us to live with dignity and hope.

We use the word *love* to cover a multitude of relationships. So, I am talking about the whole lot from enduring friendships and fickle blood-ties to romantic, passionate and unrestrained lovers. There are many nuances though, which we learn about through trial and error. We understand the meaning of these variations, in the light of prevailing circumstances. As a result *love* is a fantastic word: with many layers of meaning.

I will say more about the meaning of *love* (below). Suffice to say; while we cannot successfully dissect love into its constituent parts as though it was a machine, there are common themes. Whether it is two or more people, love is a special circle or community of relationships. In these circles, there is an intimate connection between members, where they recognize and affirm the value of the other. This involves the heart and the will for, as a loved one elicits an emotional response from us, our goodwill is also engaged for the sake of the other. We value them. We want the best for them. Even in romantic love, with a circle of two, there is a strong element of goodwill. It is what the American ethicist Margaret Farley calls "Just love". This implies that, while there may be nights of unbridled passion, where we find ourselves hanging from the chandeliers quaffing champagne, we still want to do *the right thing* by our lover. In the heat of passion, we may prefer to don leathers and stilettos, but if our partner is uncomfortable, then we will gladly abandon our accoutrements.

Our response to loved ones has a numinous quality about it, that is, the other elicits from within us a sense of wonder. With Sally, of spin the bottle fame, the transition from liking to loving hinged on this mutual evocation of wonder. This is similar to the transition from mere acquaintance to a good friend. We can know them for years, but the evocation of wonder means that it is a new relationship. It is new because we see the other differently. It is a rite of passage, which can happen in the twinkling of an eye. It is what anthropologists call a *liminal* (threshold) experience, which occurs when we cross a boundary by means of an event or ritual, such that we have a new and heightened awareness of ourselves and the world.

There is something sacred about loving relationships. By sacred, however, I do not mean that there is any hocus pocus. I mean that others, and the sheer pleasure of the relationship, evoke a sense of wonder. This is often expressed as surprise or delight like "Who *is* this remarkable person?" It has to do with seeing the other as unique, irreplaceable and precious; a real one-off. Call it *the wow factor*. But there are limits.

We know them intimately, but they are separate persons. We cannot take them over, control them or make them ours. We do not want to as the other is not a plaything, or a means to an end. Significantly, there is union and separation. While we value similarities, their otherness is part of the charm. This charm is part of what it means to say that there is something profoundly spiritual, in the broadest sense of that term, about our relationship.

I have presented a sketch of the horizon of love. This could be done in other ways, and I have not covered all the dimensions of love. So, while love does not solve all problems, it changes the way we see the people concerned, the problems raised and the nature of our responses. It is a whole person response to others, which evokes a sense of wonder and engages heart and will. And it changes us.

The Impact of Love

All those years ago, when I was playing spin the bottle, there was an intricate blend of feelings and motives that cannot be idly dismissed as puppy love. As if to say, because the experience was clumsy and tentative, there was no substance. It is true that immaturity was part of my first romantic experience, but that does not take away from the fact that for a brief, fragile moment, I was in love with Sally. Is the adult experience of love so different? Is love less nerve racking or clumsy because we are older and supposedly wiser? A good sign of the early stages of romantic love is that we are not cool or in control. Yet we often describe such behavior in self-deprecatory terms like "Goodness me, I am behaving like a teenager". In fact, love is inherently subversive as it messes with our neat plans. As a result, the teenage experience of love is arguably a more transparent, if not, a more honest account of love.

Simply put, the work of love invites us to take others seriously, such that real people become more important than abstract dogma or moral principles. Ironically, in taking others seriously we are re-born as they bring out something new in us. We see others with new eyes. We see, understand, and even love them for the first time. It may not happen instantaneously, but there is a discernible shift in the way we relate to people. Naturally, there is more to love than reflecting on a game of spin the bottle. But personal experiences like these shape our understanding of love. They act as springboards to a deeper understanding.

The cutting edge for the love horizon derives from the insight gleaned from my experience of re-visiting Christianity. This will be developed in Chapter 3. In short, love is an essential ingredient in a Christian view of life. From a Christian perspective, love is non-negotiable. It is perhaps the only *rule*. While this does not mean life's quandaries are easily resolved, if they are resolved at all, it does mean we see people differently. Radically different. Once we see people differently, we open ourselves up to the possibility of deep and lasting change. This is love upside down. So the injection of a Christian perspective of love enriches and expands the development of the love horizon. It provides content and impetus. With love as the horizon, we have a framework which makes sense of life, because it has the capacity to provide new bearings, as it incorporates and values real people. Ultimately, it affects the way we see ourselves, others and the world. It changes us. It enables and empowers us to do the work of love. The world, however, is not perfect and sometimes we fall for love-substitutes instead of real love.

2

LOVE-SUBSTITUTES

Life is messy. Life's blots, blemishes, marks and stains cannot be bleached away, because they are part of the fabric. This means life is strangely beautiful, sometimes brutal and always untidy. This is particularly true of families.

Many families use the language of love prolifically, in spite of the facts. A significant fact about many families, and a lot of relationships, is that we seldom take the kind of risks that foster fulfilling and creative expressions of love. Instead, we settle for *love-substitutes*, which are things, events or situations that masquerade as the real thing.

I have to admit, however, that I have succumbed to the charm of a love-substitute or two in my life. I too have been seduced by the spin, gloss and glitter of the world. Often it is been fun; but it didn't last. So in the name of love, let's out the impostors and prepare the way for a love to emerge that is real, big-hearted and inherently subversive.

A Christmas Caprice

This is a bad way to start Christmas. Unfortunately, I have been cornered by my Uncle Fred. Straight away, Fred proceeds to tell me for the seventh year in a row that directly after the war there was a desperate shortage of roofing iron. Inexplicably, I blurt out "That must have been tough". This is a fatal mistake; as it is the perfect segue for Fred to roar back like a wounded lion, "I'll tell you about tough pal". In keeping with Christmas, he insists on calling me pal and then proceeds to regale me with a host of stories, concluding with the one about him fighting a bushfire in 1959 and singlehandedly saving the City of Sydney from being razed to the ground. But even Fred needs to use the bathroom; so I manage to escape, only to fall into the clutches of Aunt Mavis. Mavis insists on dying her hair jet black, because she doesn't want people to know she's 83. Unfortunately, she looks like she's wearing an army helmet, circa World War 2. Proudly, she still has her own teeth.

Mavis proceeds to hug the living daylights out of me. My first cousin Adrian, who is standing beside me, grimaces as he readies himself for a frontal attack by Mavis. I am very fond of Adrian. He is a delightful human being. And this year, he has bravely brought along his partner Vincent to the family Christmas dinner. In anticipation, I wince as Mavis asks Adrian on cue "Haven't you met a nice girl yet?" Still reeling from Mavis's assault, I begin to move away only to see my second cousin Julia making a grand entrance; everyone else simply walks in.

Julia processes into the room with that celebrity look of *yes everyone, it's me*. I can't stand her, which makes it galling and incomprehensible when I greet her with "I've missed you". We soon part, exchanging mandatory air-kisses and shrieks of "Darling, darling". By mutual but unspoken consent, we spend the rest of the day studiously avoiding each other.

The Christmas experience unfolds inexorably with copious amounts of beer, champagne, wine and food. As is customary, we eat too much and laugh about the fact that we eat too much. It seems funny at the time, partly because of the wine-induced euphoria.

The grandchildren proceed to hand out gifts. Like drawing teeth, this time-honored ritual takes forever. To make matters worse, and in keeping with tradition, someone pipes up with the yuletide benediction, "The little ones are more interested in the wrapping paper than the presents". We all laugh wildly.

Ah yes, once more its aftershave, socks, underpants and monogrammed handkerchiefs for me. Ah yes, it is Christmas, which makes it all the worse that no one, not a soul, mentions my sister Janet's conspicuous absence, let alone her nervous breakdown. If her name comes up in conversation, by tacit agreement, we callously dismiss Janet's well-being with a euphemism "It's her nerves". She is *persona non grata*. But here is the punch line: Janet's exclusion is a scathing indictment of the family dinner. In this setting, the use of the word *love* has been drained of meaning.

Janet's exclusion is in fact a denunciation of the Christmas dinner. She is outside the circle. She is not treated with respect. She is a source of embarrassment rather than wonder. While the family is physically present, love is absent. In contrast, there can be a sense of love in some dysfunctional families, which sustains them in spite of the prevailing chaos. In the Christmas caprice, however, the mess is hidden, subterranean. While the family comprises a set of significant relationships in which there is shared history and knowledge that *we are family*, goodwill has gone.

The fact that a group of people make up a *family* is no guarantee that love is present. In this instance, the family chose to exclude Janet because of her mental illness and to pretend that Adrian was not gay. They were different, and while the differences were never spoken about, decisions were made about them on the basis of the differences. The scary thing is that this sort of exclusion is often executed in families without a word being spoken. Clearly, difference is a problem and everyone suffers. On the one hand, Adrian and Janet are abused by being excluded. On the other hand, the family is impoverished, because their fear of difference means that they are not open to the personal gifts that Adrian and Janet would bring to the family. Inevitably, avoidance of the real issues means it is easy for us to settle for love-substitutes.

Like a Movie Star

Relationships are complex. For good measure, we can throw into this mix: illness, loneliness, depression, punitive bosses, insuperable mortgages, infidelity, divorce, disease, death and bereavement. There's also the global financial crisis, terrorism, wars, poverty and climate change. In reality, the world is many-sided, muddled and hazardous. Do not get me wrong. There are some wonderful human beings and beautiful things. But from time to time, it is important to take a reality check. Such a check makes us realize that life is complex and there are no life-time guarantees, binding absolutes or clear-cut answers. Any moment now we could be hit by the proverbial bus. To cope effectively in running life's gauntlet, we develop common sense rules and customs like: I will be kind to animals, work hard, save money, go to gym, and eat fruit and vegetables. But rules and routines do not always work. We cannot pre-empt life's mishaps and tragedies. On the whole, the complexity and contingency of life makes love even more desirable, but it also makes us even more vulnerable to love-substitutes.

Years ago, I remember buying a very expensive suit in a fit of insanity. I rationalized the exercise by saying that it was for a special occasion and my good suit was well over 10 years old. As I left the store, I found myself glancing furtively at my reflection in the store window, thinking I was looking pretty cool. I could not help myself. It was intoxicating and I was pathetic. There I was a middle aged man, with grey hair and arthritic knees, thinking I looked like Daniel Craig, Hugh Jackman or maybe, just maybe, George Clooney. This was in spite of the lack of any corroborating evidence. But hang on a minute; Daniel, Hugh, George and I had the same suit. Yes, the very same suit. Clearly, by purchasing this suit my life had changed, because I was now a member of the in-group. Ah yes, I was seduced by a love-substitute (and I thought I was street-wise).

The in-group is an elite cluster bound together by things like money, status and a shared commitment to making sure it controls group membership. Now this group may not actually exist as a formal group, certainly not as a homogenous cluster in a certain time and place. As if Daniel, Hugh and George are knocking down gin and tonics at a fashionable cafe in Malibu, as we speak. In reality, it is about our perceptions and our needs. At the social level, the proliferation of the goods and trappings of consumer society raise serious questions about social justice, in terms of the distribution of wealth, and the treatment of workers in developing nations. At the psychological level, the fact that we can be influenced and manipulated by the creation of certain perceptions, by the promise of being *in*, gives us an insight into a poverty of spirit that plagues our era.

The culture of the in-group is related to the cult of celebrity. The celebrity is the glittering icon of the in-group, because the celebrity embodies the values and aspirations of the in-group. The celebrity is *in* because he/she is fashionable, famous and wealthy. The inescapable inference is that celebrities must be worth emulating, because other celebrities seek them out. For example, the annual Academy Awards presentation is a celebration of celebrity that is powered by the two-headed monster: the lure of being in and the fear of being out. The paparazzi, cleavage, bling, petrified hair and to-die-for handbags are signs you have made it. Strangely, it is addictive viewing. But after I have watched the Awards, a creeping sadness comes over me. It is like the end of a session of comfort eating: it felt good at the time. But it is just another love-substitute.

It is unwise to underestimate the power of being *in* and its influence. While sociologists, philosophers and theologians have examined this power from afar, the advertising gurus have instinctively exploited it. In some ways, advertising and marketing gurus have a more realistic assessment of human nature than earnest scholars. The power of being *in* is brilliant; sinister but brilliant. Remember my new suit? I grew up in a working class home where we spent much of our time trying to convince ourselves that status did not matter. But sadly, inverted snobbery means the snobs are winning. There is, nonetheless, a perverse irony in all this, as the power of the in-group is premised on the fact that we are not in. This is the source of the attraction. It is because we feel that we are *out* that we buy. Recall the painful childhood experience of not being chosen? Remember being overlooked for the school play or a hockey game? Looking back we may have coped with the rejection by saying that drama or sport is meaningless. But it hurts. So instead of dealing with the hurt, what do we do? While further down the food chain than movie stars, we still try to break into other in-groups. It is just another form of love-substitute.

The promise gets us every time. Some people, who vociferously denounce the in-group, do so because they are not in, but the nature of the protest can reveal a longing to be in. Yes it is the whim, the muffled sigh that gives it away. The whim to be in is the thing. The whim is the opening note of a personal and collective lament for the experience of wholeness. It is the human song giving voice to vulnerability. Manipulative parents, greedy media magnates, conniving marketing gurus, psychopathic bosses and schoolyard bullies all know how to identify and exploit the inner song. We need to listen to the whim.

The whim is a metaphor for our search for meaning and our need for community. In particular, most of us want to belong. This need to belong, which is a primal need for social beings, is a point of vulnerability. Moreover, if the question of vulnerability is not addressed, then we run the risk of pursuing false leads and false hopes that exploit genuine aspirations. Unless we face vulnerability, then we are sitting ducks for the next love-substitute that comes our way. Some of our needs *may* be met in the short term by love-substitutes, but the question of what it means to be a whole person in the real world is neglected. Ironically, vulnerability to love-substitutes may be an indicator that we expect too little, and not enough from life. In fact, expecting too little is a potent symbol of our impotent epoch, which values style over substance, panache over character, fame over integrity.

By all means, we should subject Christianity to a thorough-going appraisal, but this does not mean we should acquiesce to the mediocrity and self-absorption of our own era. In the context of an exploration and celebration of love, we need to cast a critical eye over the world we live in and ask what is going on. The avoidance of the big issues in human relationships like living with vulnerability, addressing difference and speaking openly about how difficult it is to do all these things, are signs of a vacuum. Something has to fill it; perhaps that's why I purchased an outrageously priced suit. Certainly, the overabundance of love-substitutes is a sign of a poverty of spirit.

The Elephant in the Sitting Room

It is not so much the money, possessions or prestige, as it is the promise of getting *in* that draws us in. The promise has an irresistible power. Look at how we portray people with status and wealth as cultural icons. What's more, all this is presented as the only option worth pursuing. The dark side of the promise is the dread of not being *in*, which means we are vulnerable, and vulnerability is the elephant in the sitting room.

Popular culture has rightly recognized that we need love, but it is usually an insipid form of love that is promoted, which fails to address the issue of human vulnerability. What I call *the love-industry* has unearthed a heartfelt need for love and that's why there is a global industry peddling love on websites, blogs, in books, songs, commercials and sitcoms. After all, why do self-help books sell like hot cakes? Why do people consult clergy, doctors, therapists, mentors, life-coaches and hairdressers? It is love. Love is not the only reason, but it is a big one. So, while the love-industry has made some positive contributions, by its very nature it runs the risk of being the worst love-substitute of all. It generally promotes an individualistic, short-term, overly-positive, quick-fix solution, with soothing-words and easy-steps. What kind of love are they selling, if it does not address the experience of vulnerability? One-dimensional, short-term attempts at addressing painful and complex problems accomplish very little. While the love-industry correctly identifies the need for love, it doesn't take love seriously enough.

Love is discovered and expressed through belonging. This raises the question of human vulnerability, because how we deal with vulnerability partly determines the nature of our relationships. These days, everyone seems to be getting in touch with their vulnerability, but the current over-use of the word *vulnerability* is off-putting. By vulnerability, I do not mean acting like an emotional doormat or telling our entire life story to everyone we meet. It is these associations which dissuade some people from seriously considering the significance of the experience of vulnerability. Vulnerability is a serious business and the inability to live with it means that there is an increased susceptibility to settling too easily for love-substitutes.

When we are vulnerable, it is more often than not because we have been dragged in by life, kicking and screaming, against our will. As a consequence, we feel unzipped. Raw, stark naked. That's what it means to be vulnerable and this kind of vulnerability is linked to suffering; that is if I am vulnerable then I can be hurt. That's why the defenses go up. Sometimes that is the right thing to do. But if we keep the defenses up all the time, in order to avoid suffering, we cut ourselves off from love and choose instead to live under the horizon of fear.

Suffering is partly about the experience of physical pain, but it is more than that. A person undergoing chemotherapy can experience a great deal of physical suffering before, during and after treatment, but this does not capture the depth of suffering. Hair loss, resulting from chemotherapy, is a symbol of the loss of dignity and the loss of self. Above all, it is a measure of the depth of human suffering. This depth of suffering is similar to what the French Jewish philosopher Simone Weil refers to as *affliction*. It is at the point of affliction that we experience the sharp end of vulnerability. This, however, is the kind of vulnerability that makes love possible. This vulnerability is a courageous, unapologetic openness to others and the world, where we lower our defenses, live with our humanity and contribute generously to the lives of others. In reality, the capacity to live with vulnerability is an indispensable feature of the horizon of love.

3

UPSIDE DOWN

I am at risk of sounding earnest, even pompous, as I name and expel today's love-substitutes with the enthusiasm and proficiency of the Inquisition. Indeed, there is nothing more deflating in the entire world than a middle-aged killjoy. If I have erred in my ardor, however, it is because I am learning to love, finally. It is liberating. Defining it, however, is a difficult exercise.

For a start, our experience of love is often ridiculous. So while it makes sense to live the way of love, the way of love is convoluted. There is no map. This is a sobering reminder for all those people who think they can put love under a microscope, or on a spreadsheet, and identify its constituent parts. As if we can organize love.

Ironically, while the Church as an institution is a problem, I have learnt some fantastic things about love by re-visiting Christianity. Certainly, I have had to throw some things out, but I have been able to re-claim a lot about love from Christianity. I will now explore a little further the nature of the human predicament and then concentrate on the theme of love that has been shaped by the wisdom of Jesus and his understanding of the subversive kingdom of God.

Traffic on the Road

All sorts of forces and fashions bear upon us, as we seek to live life with a sense of purpose. Along the way, we may encounter love. The word love is surcharged with all sorts of connotations: good, bad and bland. But when it comes to expressing the best of what it means to be human, love is the best of all possible words. In the right situation, at the right time, the word is a gift.

Love can make adults run bare-footed through a field of flowers, sing from a mountain top or giggle like a child. The experience of love can make us alive and whole. For young and old, black and white, rich and poor, love is good, love is in demand and to our amazement love is often freely given. But real love costs; it costs a great deal because in order to experience relationships of mutual trust and respect, we need to be vulnerable. If we are vulnerable, then we will probably experience suffering, even *affliction*. So, love is complex.

I remember the first time I told my father that I loved him. After a misspent youth, I returned to the fold keen to make amends. It was not so much guilt, though that was present, but more a sense of remorse for what I had done to them. They were not saints, but they were decent, hardworking people of inestimable value. In many ways, I suspected that my father had suffered the most. It was hard to tell. While Dad cared, it was not easy for him to disclose the mysteries of the heart. But he cared. And looking back, perhaps he cared too much.

In preparation, I began rehearsing for this rite of passage by saying out loud, "I love you Dad", "Gosh I love you" and "Do you know how much I love you?" None of them felt right. While I wasn't going to make a speech, I very much wanted to say the right words. They had to be from the heart; without adornment. It was a daunting task; especially as I feared that the ensuing silence would be unbearable. Sometimes in families, it is not the words but the silence that kills. I always found it hard to read his silence.

One evening, Dad was driving me up the street to catch a train. It was a short drive. Maybe 10 minutes. Silently I began to rehearse, still searching vainly for the right words. As we got

27

closer to the station, I started to feel hot and short of breath. I began to perspire freely, so much so that he asked me tenderly "Are you okay?" "No problem" I chirped back. Feeling uncomfortable with my clumsy reply, I followed this in a more measured way with the patently brilliant response, "There is a lot of traffic on the road" (where else would it be?). I should have stopped there, but I could not help myself. Suspecting Dad had missed my pearl of wisdom, I said with even greater conviction "Yes, a lot of traffic".

As we pulled up at the lights, only seconds remained. Without thinking, I threw the door open and began to disembark. The car had not completely stopped. I was half way out, moving in a slow-motion stupor when Dad looking bemused said "See you later". A nanosecond left and I was in two minds. Staring at the sidewalk and looking at Dad, I blurted out "I love you Dad". We paused. The silence was bearable, apposite, even comforting. I shut the door, paused again and then sped off into the night like a gazelle.

It is crazy that we find it so hard to express our love to loved ones. Is it a male thing? Well I am not sure, especially when I listen to my female friends, who reassure me that it is not ginger-peachy for them either. When I told Dad, it was a mixture of the ordinary, the extraordinary and the absurd, all of which evoked fear and elation in equal measure. But I never regretted saying those words. I have said it since then, many times, but it is not the same. More recently, I have been guilty of excess as I have tried in vain to love this good man back to life. The first time I said it to him was messy, but it was perfect. Just perfect. It was a rare gift, a half-chance to respond to this irreplaceable man and a reminder of what real love is like.

Real love is irreducible, disruptive and redeeming. It is a pathway to a deeper life with an inherently new perspective on ourselves, others and the world. This perspective creates a new attitude. The word *attitude*, however, as in the expression *she's got attitude* can mean that she is a pain in the neck. Alternatively, it can mean that she is spirited as in "I like her attitude". It is in this vein that a love-filled life is a life lived with a gritty, take-the-world-on attitude. It is a positive robust energy, which is willing to drop defenses and move bravely into intimate and open spaces where love is born, nurtured and strengthened. In other words, we are emboldened to move out of our caves, clubs, coteries and cloisters into the world, with a generosity of heart and spirit that is grounded in a passion for life and a compassion for others. Ultimately, this is real love.

The idea of a loving person can sound soppy, but the work of love is not insipid. The emboldened lover is not looking for a re-assuring hug, although she is not afraid to ask for one. Actually, someone who is committed to the way of love possesses a certain kind of daring. She has to because her actions will not always be popular; especially as she embraces others who are different. Ironically, popularity is not a consideration. So in spite of its problems, its inherent ambiguity and its susceptibility to misuse, I am putting *love* forward as the horizon by which we both look at life and live out our lives.

But love is not always like this in wider society, especially in the movies. To be honest, when a couple makes love in the movies there is no "I need to go to the bathroom", "Please move your arm" or "Where are the tissues?" In the movies, there is no embarrassed giggling or post-coital snoring. In the movies, children sleep through the night. What's more, there is often an absence of fear and fear is an important dimension of real love.

Fear goes hand in hand with love. Now this is not a demeaning comment about the nature of love, or the character of our loved ones. Quite the opposite: this is recognition that there is a type of fear that surfaces when you least expect it, when ordinary people make love or are in love. It is that sense of wonder which often finds its true expression in benign incredulity, like "Where did that come from?" It comes from the deep, our core. It happens when what makes us human is touched. It is chilling, because we are unzipped (and now everyone can peer inside and see what we are really like). Be that as it may, while the state of being figuratively unzipped makes us vulnerable to suffering, it is also the ground for being renewed and refashioned by love. But let's explore the idea of making love.

Making love is a beguiling expression. We know what it means; we do not need a map. But first let's think about the term *make*. When a couple *makes* love, what does that mean? The word has a number of possibilities like build, compose, construct, create or form. In the expression *making love, make* is used in the sense of create. So, on the one hand, making love is not like planning to go out to the shed to build a coffee table. It is not a scheduled task, but a spontaneous and creative action. Typically, it may begin with flowers and champagne and end with a riotous evening of unrestrained passion. But there is no guarantee of how the night will go. If the chemistry is right, it just happens. On the other hand, there is a sense in which we make it happen, that is we work. Like the coffee table exercise, there is intention and commitment to the work, because emotion includes a value-judgment about the other person and the relationship itself. The whim becomes a virtue. Usually, but not always, commitment to the work of love enables the relationship to thrive, often enhancing and enriching the passionate moments. So the idea of work, of *making* love, says something about our regard for the other person as well as our personal integrity. The work of love then is not solely the logical outcome of a night of passion, it is also a corollary of how we *feel* about and *regard* (value) the other person.

We are talking about real life, which is complicated and contingent. It is complicated because our life, our real life, is intertwined with the lives of others: with their own, sometimes conflicting, often conflicted, take on reality. It is contingent on a raft of things, known and unknown, manageable and ungainly.

When we talk about love, it is not against a Hollywood backdrop with body doubles, soft lighting and computer enhancement. It is about reality. It is about creativity and work; that is the creativity of an artist and the work of a laborer. This work encompasses romantic love, friendship, various movements of people, and inspired faith communities committed to love. In this sense, love is not only a delight, but it is also part of the human vocation. This is precisely what gives us a new perspective on others, who like us are embroiled in the dilemmas and complexities of the real world.

I am working out of a faith perspective. By *faith perspective*, I do not mean religious fundamentalism of any persuasion. There's no Bible thumping here. I am writing specifically out of a Christian perspective, but I am aware that even a passing reference to Christianity can scare off some readers. Be assured that when it comes to God, I do not believe there is an old man in the sky controlling world events. I will say more about this later. And while I respect the other religions of the world, I am focused on the Christian view of God. Even so, we still need to deal with Christianity's baggage before we look at its under- standing of the horizon of love.

Excess Baggage

To recap, we are exploring the theme of love, where love is the horizon, which galvanizes heart and mind to do the work of love. This work invites us to take others seriously. Ironically, in taking others seriously, we see others with new eyes and we are renewed in the process. We see, appreciate and love them for the first time. Now this may sound like new age love-speak or psycho-babble except for two things. First, it is grounded in real life. There's no gilding of the lily. Second, it is inspired and informed by some ancient yet radical insights that stem directly from Christianity. By radical, I do not mean anything like blanket contempt for *the establishment*. I mean radical, in the sense of getting to the root of things, such that we are transformed from the inside out. This is love upside down.

I am not captive to Christianity, but it is the path I choose to follow. I could not follow it, however, until I confronted and ejected some excess baggage. Certainly, I know a great deal about Christianity's failings and its interminable struggle with power and privilege. But I have also met magnanimous faith communities too, full of courageous and generous lovers. What's more, we are kidding ourselves if we think we can avoid the problems of institutions, as if the Church is the only problematic institution. The real issue is *healthy* institutions, which are human and humane; open to examination, criticism and change. In fact Christianity, with its take on love, has a major contribution to make. But I need to say something about what I mean by *Christianity*, because it comes with baggage.

To do this, I will illustrate something of the prevalence of stereotypes about Christianity, so that we can talk about the real thing. This involves looking at the idea of *spirituality*. I will then spell out four criteria for making sure that when we talk about Christianity, we are talking about the real thing.

Imagine walking through Central Park, enjoying the sun on a glorious spring day. In the distance, there is a group of people performing *Tai Chi*. It is an enchanting scene as the assembled company, consisting of diverse racial and cultural groups, are moving as one. Effortlessly, the quiet and graceful dignity of the individuals forms a harmonious unity. While we are not entirely sensitive to the spiritual nuances of *Tai Chi*, we are touched by this reverent and refined display. Full of admiration for the participants, we find ourselves thinking, "Maybe there's cause for hope in the world". Wistfully, we leave the group and continue walking deeper into the park.

Eventually, we come to another gathering, also consisting of different racial and cultural groups. In this situation, however, the individuals are kneeling in a circle; each with theirs hands clasped and looking vacantly toward the sky. "Oh no, it's a bunch of weirdo Christians brazenly praying, hoping to convert clueless passersby. This is embarrassing. Why can't they keep their religion to themselves?" This second group, however, may not be a bunch of wacko Christians. It is conceivable that here is a group of sane and compassionate Christians, meditating together, trying to still their hearts and minds before preparing to cook and serve a hot meal to hundreds of homeless people.

The point of the comparison is that, in the West, it is difficult to look at Christian images, symbols and rituals, without prejudice. Spiritually, the ethereal wisdom of the East is in and the religious drivel of the West is out. Significantly, the stereotype of Christianity being entirely composed of religious *fruitcakes* is part of the baggage, which prevents many people from revisiting Christianity and seeing what it has to say about love. So before we can proceed unencumbered, a few more remarks need to be made about some of the other pieces of Christian baggage. To begin, a classic piece of baggage is that Christianity is primarily about religion and not about spirituality. So, on that count alone, it is worth exploring the term *spirituality*.

There is no simple or universal definition of the word *spirituality*. Like the word *love*, spirituality is irreducible and that is both its strength and its weakness. The weakness of the word *spirituality* is that it can mean almost anything you like. In the Church, some have tried to define spirituality in highly prescriptive terms in order to use it as a basis for discrediting alternative beliefs or practices. This is the *Father knows best* syndrome, which means that the bishop or priest has all the answers and by inference, everyone else is an idiot. In fairness, however, Christianity has not cornered the market on religious know-alls, control freaks or shysters. Actually, anything you like can masquerade today as spirituality. If you have a spare year, check out the word *spirituality* on the web. Clearly, there are many new, savvy and exciting ventures into alternative spiritualities, which are meeting the needs of a growing throng of individuals. The Church can learn from these movements. In addition, I suspect *the perception* that the Church has failed to act in a loving manner has fueled this growth. All the same, there are countless self-help charlatans and new age gurus outside the Church, peddling snake oil and quick-fix remedies to a gullible public. Remember *Chance the gardener* in the film *Being There*? He spoke literally about gardening, but his dull snippets were construed as brilliant parables. The genius of the film is found in its portrayal of how easily people falsely attributed wisdom and insight to Chance, who was a simple-minded man.

The strength of the word *spirituality*, however, captures what many people feel instinctively. It is the whence of the whim. It is the space where the melody of the soul is born. It affirms that, while institutions need to be approached with caution, personal experience has not lost its value or appeal. All sorts of people grasp the meaning of spirituality. It is like "Spirituality? I get it, I just don't get religion". But institutions are unavoidable.

Let's examine briefly the contribution Christianity can make to our exploration of love, in the context of recognizing the shortcomings of the Church and the renewed interest in spirituality. First, Christianity should not be dismissed out of hand, on the basis of the princely attitude of some of its leaders or the extreme behavior of its fundamentalist fringe, just as the new age interest in spirituality should not be treated dismissively because of its superficial or money-making manifestations. Beware of stereotypes, of all persuasions.

Second, Christianity has something vital to contribute to our exploration of love. By Christianity's contribution, I do not mean innocent answers from Sunday school days. I am talking about an adult understanding of faith. I am not including the alarming images of fundamentalist preachers, which we find on our televisions and in our tabloids that conspire to inoculate us against re-visiting Christianity.

Third, Christianity has important insights, but it does not have the whole truth. I do not think that any individual or institution can seriously lay claim to the whole truth, because that sounds a lot like playing God.

Fourth, by Christianity, I am not talking about the traditional view of God, which theologians and philosophers refer to under the broad title of *theism*. In essence, theism is the idea that God created the world, but remains separate, while retaining the capacity to intervene in human affairs and world events. In its naïve form, this is *the old man in the sky* or the *Mr. Fix-it-God*. The problem with this view is that the God in question does not seem to fix anything. While there are many reasons for questioning traditional theism, it is the problem of suffering that raises the tough questions (see my book *I Met God in Bermuda*). In short, from war to earthquakes, how can a loving God let these things happen?

The experience of suffering shows the limits of traditional theism in the contemporary world and underlines some of the reasons why Christianity is, in various quarters, reinventing itself. Now, while this is not a theological text book, it is important that I am transparent about my assumptions. For me, God is neither an old man in the sky nor a human invention. God sits on the edge of reality and is discovered by us in our relationships, in particular, in and through our experience of love. God is love and love is God. Every time I re-visit Christianity, all this becomes more apparent and more powerful. Love is all that matters. That's the heart of the Christian message.

Sex was a No-No

Our understanding of love involves our understanding of sex, but sex has been a problem in the West. Many of us have been brought up to think that sex is inherently naughty, if not evil. It is the great stain on our collective character. Throughout Western history, sex has been presented, overtly and covertly, as a form of personal or cultural sullying. Much popular humor has been premised on this indelible stain, from the title of a long running West End farce "No sex please – we're British" to Woody Allen's quip "Is sex dirty? Only if it's done right". But the stain has permeated many aspects of life. When we were young, for example, why did mother stand in front of the television, with skirt fanned wide, shielding her brood from the unexpected appearance of a bare-breasted woman in a vaguely exotic European movie? More importantly, why did our parents find it hard to talk to us about sex?

I can only recall one conversation on the topic of sex with either of my parents. It was with Dad. Once again, we were in the car. I am not sure why our significant exchanges took place in the car, but I guess there is something safe about a car journey. It is this unusual mix of the cone of silence and the confessional, which permits free association. I look back on these times with affection as they were incandescent moments in a dull suburban life. The conversations were artless, invariably roundabout, but they often touched the heart. Surprisingly it was Dad, that uniquely Australian blend of the laconic and the stoical, who initiated this particular encounter. When he began, it didn't register for a while what he was talking about. The topic had something to do with the biological changes I was about to undergo as a pubescent teenager. Thankfully, the conversation petered out. We were both nervous and looking straight ahead, out the front window, as though something vital was taking place on the road. I felt embarrassed, a little flushed actually, but I managed to restrain myself from saying something stupid.

Despite my father's best efforts, sex was a no-no. The cultural tide was against us, so that most of us learnt little about the largely unmentionable things like sexual intercourse, mastur-bation or menstruation. Even if parents dared to leave sexually explicit magazines on the coffee table for us to stumble on, it only reinforced the notion that sex was a no-no. As a result, it is obvious that we cannot begin to address the themes of sex and love with a shred of open-mindedness, unless we name this heritage of shame and guilt. As the French philosopher Paul Ricoeur observed "an indissoluble complicity between sexuality and defilement seems to have been formed since time immemorial". This is in no small part the result of the Church's fixation with a particular type of moral purity, which is often cloaked under the seemingly respectable mantle of *orthodoxy*.

The Rhetoric of Orthodoxy

Sex can be a powerful expression and affirmation of love. It is a gift. It is one of the great pleasures of life; better than a citron tart with real coffee on the left bank in Paris. But when it comes to discussing sex, terms like *the orthodox tradition* or *orthodoxy* are often used in a negative manner to restrict, control or terminate the conversation. Repeatedly, in Christian forums, the mantle of *orthodoxy* is played like a trump card as in "This is the orthodox position". So that is the end of the matter. Who would dare question or challenge orthodoxy? Of course, only a heretic would make such a challenge. While the term *heretic* is rarely uttered, it is implied by the use of leading questions like "Of course, you do support the orthodox position of the universal Church?"

While we do not want to get bogged down in a theological quagmire, it is important to have a grasp of the meaning of these terms. Specifically, it is useful to look at the use of the term *orthodoxy*. In a nutshell, the term *orthodoxy* means right opinion (or true belief). In itself, this is a good thing. Clearly, most of us would like to live by right opinions. The problem, however, is three-fold: what is right, who says so and on what basis? On historical grounds alone, the orthodox position is not always patently clear. Historically, the so-called seamless orthodox tradition has been patched together. As a result, there are four issues which need to be mentioned now, so that we can continue our exploration of love with greater clarity.

First, from the second century, and under the influence of several ideas (neo-Platonism, Manichaeism), a negative view of the body and sexual relations began to permeate the thinking and culture of the Church. In this view, the body is regarded as separate from and inferior to the spirit. The spirit must be saved, because the body is tainted. This was more than just an isolated opinion as it became the broad horizon against which spirit and body, male and female, love and sex, were all judged. Before this era, there were some negative attitudes toward the body and sex, but they did not necessarily form an all-encompassing horizon. What's more, in a Jewish setting, these negative instances were counterbalanced by the notion that humankind, the body and sexuality were gifts from God (Genesis 1; Psalm 8). From this perspective, and this is also true of the apostle Paul, we talk about the whole person as a unity of body *and* spirit. The whole person then, including the body, is worthy of respect.

Second, the so-called orthodox Christian tradition has promoted the institution of marriage as *the template* for adult relationships. But the character, practice and status of marriage have evolved since the first century. For example, the modern conception of marriage does not include the first century practice of a betrothal period. Likewise, the cult of virginity, which was held in esteem in the early centuries, meant celibacy became a prized mode of existence in the middle Ages. The practice of marriage varies across cultures too; polygamy is a good example of this.

Third, the main impediment to a fresh appraisal of love has to do with the historic (read orthodox) equation of sex and procreation. The argument goes like this: sex is for making babies and you need to be married to have sex. Right or wrong, this equation has dominated Western thinking about sex. While there are ancient and authoritative sources in favor of the sex/procreation equation, ranging from biblical references to medieval theologians, the decider is the uncritical use of these sources to win an argument or control a conversation. The mere citing of revered sources does not constitute strong evidence or compelling argument. For instance, there are ancient and authoritative sources in favor of slavery, but we reject slavery on the basis of new evidence and fresh arguments. These fresh arguments are compelling in their own right, but they also have a certain gravitas, because we go back and analyze afresh the traditional sources as part of the process of discernment. Just because it is in the Bible, or a medieval theologian says it, does not make it right.

Fourth, the term *orthodox* has to do with right or proper belief. It is an important term, as it defines historic and shared grounds for belief. The term, without solving all theological debates, sets up broad parameters for belief, but it does not address all the existential and ethical contingencies that real people face today.

In summary, the term orthodoxy is used in two ways: technical and rhetorical. The technical use of the term *orthodoxy* incorporates views of early church councils, creeds and its leading figures. Even here, however, the emergence of the Church's understanding of orthodoxy was not straightforward. The existence of the early councils of the Church is testimony to the presence of conflict, mixed motives and diverse opinions. The technical use of the term *orthodoxy*, however, tells us a good deal about Christian belief and identity. It is the second use of orthodoxy that is the problem. The rhetorical use of the term *orthodoxy* covers all manner of things. Generally, the purpose is to persuade people about the rightness of a particular view. This is achieved at the expense of divergent views that are persuasively caricatured and summarily dismissed as liberal, progressive, humanist or secular thinking. The inference is that these latter views are unorthodox, if not heretical, and that a person of faith should have nothing to do with them. At the least, the rhetorical use of *orthodoxy* to inhibit debate, discredit opponents or prevent new examinations of old positions is not remotely a loving way to conduct a conversation.

I am arguing that sex is a gift and that the full potential of this gift is realized in the context of love. The debate, however, surrounding sex and love has been dominated by particular views of the body, sex and sexual relations, which have relied on the selective use of evidence, untested assumptions and circular argumentation. More significantly, from Augustine to Luther and the present day, there has been a reluctance to examine afresh the presumptions behind the so-called orthodox tradition. So this is not a criticism of orthodoxy per se, because at root their lies a genuine human concern about right opinion, knowledge and true belief. But it is a criticism of the use of the term *orthodoxy* to control debate or exclude other people from participating in the conversation. In that situation, the word *orthodoxy* is an ecclesiastical gobstopper. This sort of manipulation, in which the opponent is defamed, is destructive. It certainly is not Christian. In contrast, my plea is to look at the issues and the conduct of the debate afresh from within the love horizon. Specifically, it is a plea to look at people *as people* before we begin to set our rules in concrete. On that note, it is timely to remind ourselves of the power of love.

Agape or Eros: It's all Greek to Me

I must be in the *Guinness* book of records for having sung the sentimental favorite *O Perfect Love* the greatest number of times in recorded history. It is in the hundreds. Literally. This amazing feat occurred in the innumerable weddings that I have conducted over the years. In preparing a wedding service, I generally discourage couples who are not practicing Christians from including hymns, on the basis that few people sing in public today, let alone in church. I suggest to the couple that a poor rendition of a hymn runs the risk of detracting from the magic of the moment. In response, the bride-to-be is often uncertain. The groom, who is eager to please, grins sheepishly, but wisely remains silent. Mother, however, who has been uncharacteristically quiet, makes her presence felt. Like something from the opening scene of Macbeth, she cries out "It's *your* wedding, but you know what that hymn means to me" and adds as an afterthought "and your father too". The couple eventually gives in to Mother and so, against my better judgment, we include the hymn. Predictably, when it comes to the wedding, not a soul joins in the hymn singing. So, once again, I break into a solo performance of *O Perfect Love*. Sometimes, I get carried away as if I am Pavarotti and I really belt it out. If I am lucky, however, the organist makes it a duet. But here's the rub. In spite of this, something powerful takes place in the service that evokes a sense of wonder and delight, transforming a potential farce into a potent symbol of love.

One event stood out repeatedly. It was the reading of I Corinthians 13, which begins with "If I speak in the tongues of mortals and of angels... ". If it was read well, an irresistible calm filled the church as people listened intently. It was more than listening though. It was worship, in the best sense of that word. Even the pathological talkers paused for breath, because of the power of the moment. And when I mean read well, I am not talking about a highly polished reading by a veteran news anchor or a distinguished thespian. Often, it was a young niece who read with heart and soul, who saw the opportunity to read at her cousin's wedding as a great honor. So she practiced, and practiced the reading, until the ancient words were hers. In this setting, familiar phrases like "Love is patient" came alive with new power. You could feel it. It was palpable. When it came to the words "Love never ends" an electric current coursed through the congregation stirring us deeply and making us one. Even battle-hardened clergy were moved. Finally, the niece got to pronounce the unofficial blessing, "and the greatest of these is love". And then there was silence.

This ancient reading has power. I mean why on earth is it chosen, at countless weddings and many funerals, by people who would not describe themselves as religious? It is because it is a heady, powerful, unapologetic celebration of love. Over the millennia, readings like the niece's, as well as poems, psalms and other hymns of love have survived and surpassed the Church's frailty. For example, the theme of love shines through the so-called friendship of David and Jonathan, the story of Ruth, the Song of Songs, as well as the lives of Mary Magdalene, St Augustine, the Celtic mystics, Julian of Norwich, 17th century priest-poets, Evelyn Underhill and Desmond Tutu. Not to mention Jesus.

This tradition of love, which finds its locus in the life and teachings of Jesus, is the Church's source of resilience, relevance and integrity. It is also the defining measure of what it means to be Christian. Is it any wonder then that scholars have tried to analyze the meaning of the word *love*? Now there is a long history here, which we will look at briefly, and this is because the scholars have some good things to say. Ultimately, however, the most important analysis of love is not a linguistic turn or a philosophical insight, but a personal work. In the real world, love resides in relationships. Love is profoundly personal. It is the love that is manifested in ordinary, often fragile and sometimes heroic lives, that rings true. This personal face of love is not a distraction from the fruit of scholarly labor: on the contrary, it is the real deal. A scholarly insight about love in theory, though illuminating, is not the same as love in action. With those qualifications in place, it is important to scan the debate.

In Greek, which is the language of the New Testament, there are different words for love. By far, the main word for *love* in the New Testament is *agape*. Traditionally, this has been translated in Latin as *caritas* and in English as *charity*. The word *agape*, which has an imposing and complex history, refers to love that is associated with an act of the will. For example, it is the love that is expressed to the unlovable, on the basis of the good-will of the lover. It is love for the other, without consideration of our own needs. With *agape* love, love is a gratuitous gesture. It is not based on the merit of the recipient. It is a gift of grace, perhaps a pure gift, expecting little in return. The Italian philosopher Gianni Vattimo aptly summarizes the import of this word "The only truth revealed to us by Scripture... is the truth of love, of charity." While the followers of Jesus are expected to enact this kind of love, the word *agape* is more often than not associated with God. Unsurprisingly then, in the ancient world, *agape* was accorded greater esteem and value than say *eros*, because *agape* was of God.

In contrast, *eros* is the love of union, the union of the separated, and the sexual/spiritual union of lovers. In mystical terms, *eros* is the union of divine and human. In the mid 20th century, significant thinkers made a sharp distinction between *agape* and *eros*. According to this trend, *agape* and *eros* are irreconcilable. A marked contrast was subsequently established on the basis of this academic division: *agape* is of God but *eros* is of humankind; God loves (*agape*) expecting nothing in return but humankind loves (*eros*) expecting something in return. God's love is a gift, but the love of humankind expresses a need. God's nature is compassionate; we are bound to passion. Today many scholars, like the American theologian Carter Heyward, disagree with the idea of subdividing love. For her, the split is "a radical misapprehension of love, which is at once divine and human". As the Australian theologian John Gaden claimed, "We need a true marriage of eros and agape".

Agape and Eros: It's all Love to Me

Let's place the love debate in a broader context. While the *agape/eros* distinction makes some sense, it is not a case of either/or but both/and. This means a number of things. It says something about my approach, in that I am exploring love by taking a thematic approach; that is I am not reducing love to constituent parts. I am also skeptical about the benefits of in-depth word studies, as if love can be sliced and diced and what's left over is called true love or the truth of love. I am not saying that there is no value in these approaches, or in developing a catalog of love, but only that it is of limited value. I make this claim on the basis of how we make love in real life and how we use the word *love* in English. What's more, human relationships, human motivation and the nature of the divine-human relationship are multifaceted. The either/or approach does not do justice to this complexity.

In practice, we use the word *love* for a particular set of relationships. We say we love our partner, child, parent, sibling or friend, but normally we do not say that we love the plumber or the dentist, even if we like them. So we use the word *love* for a specific relationship, in which there is a shared regard, intensity and intention. These qualities are markers of the sacred space we share. Sometimes, as a consequence, we warm to the imperfec-tions of our loved ones. Other times, we challenge them. Further, if we move house we do not need grief counseling because we left the plumber behind (the hairdresser is an exception). But we try to maintain relationships with family and friends because of the intensity of these relationships, and the shared history. We are intentional about working on them. In this context, love is an affirmation of what is shared. Love, however, is not perfect and human motivation is never pure. So there are always elements of egoism as well as altruism. That's the way it is.

In English, and this is its strength, we use the one word *love* to convey the multifaceted nature of love. What's more, the fantastic thing about a living language is that we learn the range of meanings as we use the language in the real world. For example, young Australians currently use the word *wicked* to mean good or excellent, in the sense of delightful. While it possesses a nuance of mischief, it is mischievous in the sense of indulging an impulse, like eating chocolate. In this case, it does not mean *evil*. We know this on the basis of how we use it.

On the basis of how we use the word *love*, love is indissoluble. It is a remarkable singularity. It has a multitude of meanings and applications, but it resists dissection. We celebrate the wealth of meanings and the infinite hues of love. We do not need explicit instructions to know that in a particular situation, the love implied is romantic, familial, friendly or neighborly. Most people are capable of reading the signs most of the time. I can say to a good friend "I love you Deborah" without having to add "but I don't want to sleep with you" in case she gets the wrong idea.

Now, let's return to the love debate. Intuitively, the distinction between *agape* and *eros* makes sense. Experience has taught us that there are people out there who love us for who we are. They love us generously, selflessly and altruistically, even when we are unlovable. In contrast, there are others who *love* us as a means to an end. They are not generous but self-serving. In this instance, the name *love* is a misnomer. In human terms, however, motivation is never pure. Human beings are funny old things and our intentions and motivations are intricate. For example, so-called self-less love can be egotistical, such as the friend or family member who is *ever so humble*. In other words, the sheer intensity of his/her self-effacing behavior constitutes a form of self-absorption. In contrast, while altruistic love is not selfish, it still involves a self; but it comes out of an expanded or expansive sense of self, and that's a good thing. We use words like magnanimous or generous to describe that sense of a *bigger* self. They are the people who go the extra mile. They have a healthy sense of self, which means that love enables them to transcend self-preoccupation when it counts.

A god, understood purely in terms of *agape*, is too good, too remote and too holy. I cannot relate to this god. While I do not want a god who is like a pet cat or a designer accessory, I cannot love a god who is too good to understand, too remote to feel and too holy to handle. When it is all one way, it doesn't feel like a relationship. In fact, it is not a relationship and we run the risk of becoming God's accessory. In contrast, the mystical traditions (Celtic, medieval, romantic) teach us the joy of union with the divine. The Bible also contains literature in *The Song of Songs* (*The Song of Solomon*), which celebrates the erotic union of lovers, as well as the union of human and divine. In these biblical texts, the metaphor of *God as lover* is fitting and inspiring. No wonder these biblical references are being re-discovered and re-claimed in weddings, funerals, formal worship, private meditation and public events.

The Song of Songs makes a radical affirmation about the connection between: the divine, divine love and the love that draws lovers together in sweet embrace. At the mystical level, all love is divine; it is the glue that enables individuals to perform heroic acts, as well as sustaining troubled families and fractured communities. It gives us a sense of the sacredness of life. In contrast, while the dichotomy between *agape* and *eros* has merit, *agape* alone creates a barrier between the human and the divine. Above all else, it is too neat. *Agape* by itself does not ring true. It needs *eros*. So, with these reflections in mind, what can the Christian tradition offer to the task of developing an understanding of the horizon of love?

Life Changing; World Turning

It is important now to concentrate on the life of Jesus, in order to establish a basis for a Christian outlook on love. There is broad consensus that Jesus was passionately concerned about love. From mainstream Christians to begrudging skeptics, there is recognition that he practiced what he preached. With that in mind, let us survey his teachings and focus on the kingdom of God and the meaning of his death.

The four New Testament gospels of Matthew, Mark, Luke and John are pivotal in Christianity for helping us find our bearings on what it means to be *Christian*. The gospels, however, are the result of major editorial activity. But this does not mean that someone was sitting in a study with a notebook computer, like a modern historian, recording the facts about Jesus in an analytical and objective manner. It is a more active, more engaged process. It is more concerned with the proclamation of a renewing movement of love, which finds its locus in Jesus, than the preservation of historical facts about a dry historical figure. This means that the editorial activity took place in community, for the sake of communities. In summary, the original good news is that people matter. The different and sometimes conflicting gospel accounts do not constitute evidence proving that the editors got the facts wrong. On the contrary, the differences are evidence that the editors wrote their gospels for the needs of different faith communities. So, the sayings and stories of Jesus were woven into the weft and warp of a larger fabric for the spiritual and pastoral needs of real people and real communities.

The theme of love runs through all the gospels; this is reasonable grounds for seeing love as indispensible to the ministry of Jesus and the movement he led. For example, in the gospel of Matthew, a new era is inaugurated through the life of Jesus, which is built on the old tradition, although Jesus takes it one step further. The famous *Sermon on the Mount* is a presentation of the new way that can be summarized by one word and that is *love* (Matthew 5-7). So, the *Sermon on the Mount* is not simply a catalog of otherworldly platitudes; it is about the impact of love in the world. Love God and love your neighbor as yourself (Matthew 22:34-40). It is as simple as that. Love is the bottom line. It is the first and final measure of what can be credibly construed as *Christian* (Matthew 25:31-46). The gospel of John, written a decade later and in a different situation, also presents Jesus in the light of love. For example, Jesus' washing the feet of his disciples bears witness to the preeminence of love. In so doing, Jesus establishes a new way of relating with his followers. They are no longer servants; they are friends. Jesus' action represents a significant departure from social and religious custom. In other words, Jesus has subverted the social order, for the sake of others, all in the name of love. This is love upside down. This also becomes an important model for followers, that is, here is a benchmark for Christian behavior. These themes are also picked up in the gospel of Luke in the archetypal stories of *The Good Samaritan* and *The Prodigal* or *Lost Son*, where the extravagance of the love of God, that excess of grace and generosity of spirit, is doubly emphasized. The unexpected happens in both stories. In *The Good Samaritan* it is the foreigner (Samaritan) who does the good deed and not the respected religious figures. In *The Lost Son*, the dissolute younger son is not punished, but welcomed on his return. Again, it is not what we expected. While we enjoy these stories, they leave our heads spinning as we feel we are being drawn into something wonderful, yet powerful, which will turn our world upside down.

Undoubtedly, love is a major theme in the life of the Jesus movement. But again we have to ask: what kind of love is it? Importantly, this is not love as an abstract universal principle, but love as a concrete response by Jesus to people on the edge. This is love in action, as he embraces the unacceptable and brings them back into community. It is important to note, however, the significance of these people being *on the edge* in order to appreciate the character of the love of Jesus. These people are different (sick, mentally ill, poor, women). They are alienated from community. So, the different, the other and the unacceptable pay an additional price for their estrangement in spiritual, social and economic terms. On one level, for example, if they are sick, then pain and distress are the price. On another level, they are also stigmatized for being sick, so the price goes up as they bear the shame of being different. It is more than physical suffering. This is *affliction* as they are not fit for respectable company and they know it. Like the Christ-figure of Christian piety, marginalized people bear the stigma. A classic example of this is the woman who hemorrhaged (below).

For the Sake of Real People

In the 1st century, various Jewish groups were nurtured by a vision of a God who cared for those on the margins and offered them the hope of liberation. Of course, the debate among these groups concerned who would be set free, when it would happen and how it would be achieved. With Mary Magdalene and others, Jesus came from the north of Palestine (Galilee) as part of a movement that shared such aspirations. This comes through in his teachings on the kingdom of God (Mark 1:14-15).

To reiterate, the phrase *the kingdom of God* is critical for understanding the way of Jesus. The Greek word, which we translate as kingdom, is *basileia*. It relates to the active presence of God in the world, both now and in the future. The kingdom of God is intangible, unconventional and dynamic. It is a quirky and subversive kingdom, turning the world upside down; turning it up the right way. For convenience sake, I will use the English word *kingdom*. I will also use *the quirky kingdom* or *the reign of God*. In the end, however, you cannot pin down the kingdom of God.

All things considered, the kingdom of God is the creative impact of God in the world: now and in the future. While the *timing* differs between the gospels, the future holds decisive and transformative possibilities as the horizon of the future, informs and shapes present hopes and expectations. The impact then of the kingdom is world-transforming. It is open to everyone. It is characterized by joy, justice and a generosity of spirit. It is a kingdom of love. But how does this relate to the work of love today? This is where the symbol of the banquet comes in.

In the gospels, the banquet is both an event and a symbol of the dawning of the reign of God. This can be seen at a number of levels, which interact with each other, serving to underline the power of the banquet symbol. First, though it caused offense, Jesus chose to eat with the marginalized. Second, the banquet as metaphor shows the kingdom as countercultural because of its inclusive nature. In this perspective, the banquet is for the blind, the lame, the poor, children and women. It is for those who bear the stigma. Ironically, it is the stigmatized that see and understand the ministry of Jesus. In the Gospel of Mark, for instance, a deliberate contrast is made between the disciples who see but do not understand, and those people on the edge of society who see *and* understand. In one classic case, a blind man can see who Jesus *really* is (Mark 10:46-52). Third, in the gospel of John, Jesus uses a banquet as a means of inaugurating *a new order*, which is a new way of being and relating. In this context, it is a subversive kingdom, in that it is not the expected order of things.

In the Jesus tradition, the first shall be last and the last shall be first. This is comforting news for some, but it is unsettling for others. In the Sermon on the Mount, Jesus subverts our thinking with the piercing refrain "You have heard that it was said... but I say to you, love your enemies". Love your enemies? This is too much. But this is love upside down.

In brief, the kingdom perspective is grounded and expressed in love. The kingdom perspective changes the way we see others, so that we cannot help but see others as persons worthy of love, who are to be invited into community with joy and goodwill. Love is transformative; people are changed. Love is inclusive; people are welcomed. Love has an affinity for people on the edge; differences are embraced. And anyone with open heart and mind is able to receive this gift.

A God of Love

The horizon of love is about relationships here and now, but there is a future dimension. This means that while the present obstacles are not miraculously removed, they do not have the final say, because there is a sense of future possibilities. The experience of suffering, even *affliction*, is not the final word on human dignity. All this helps to explain the meaning of the crucifixion, which in turn becomes the definitive measure of the horizon of love. This may seem a strange thing to say: that is to conceive the crucifixion positively, especially as this ancient Christian symbol comes encrusted with notions of failure and shame. But first, let me put the crucifixion in the context of the wider Christian tradition.

With matters of faith, there is no one-size-fits-all response. Imagine placing a hundred people in a room and asking them to describe the meaning of the crucifixion in 500 words or less. I suspect we would be staggered by the range of answers given. In the Church's tradition, dogma and creeds define broad areas of agreement. They try to say what we can and cannot believe, but they do not exhaust the meaning of faith or account for the ambiguity of human experience. Moreover, the meaning of faith is discovered and claimed in and through lived experience. Experience happens; it happens all the time. As a result, the reflection and analysis of experience from the perspective of faith comes next. Ultimately, faith only makes sense in the context of the human predicament. Councils, synods and academies may offer learned or authoritative insights, but these insights are road tested in real life by individuals and faith communities.

Historically, the meaning of the cross has been explored on the basis of various theories of atonement. But please do not tune out here. This is not arid or obtuse theology. It is life-related because it raises the question of what our god is really like and, in the process; it tells us something about the character of our spiritual life. So it has practical implications. Besides it shows how Christianity, despite its failings, is grounded in love.

The term *atonement* refers to both the belief that the cross brought about reconciliation between God and humanity and the explanation as to how this was achieved. In some instances, atonement theories have portrayed God as aggrieved, demanding, wrathful or deficient in some way, requiring a sacrifice or demanding satisfaction. But what kind of a god is this? What kind of god wills a death? It is not my god. What is more, the onus in this view is on Jesus, in his death, meeting God's needs. But there are other ways of looking at the cross, where the onus is on Jesus, in his life, expressing God's love. In the latter view, the cross is the outworking of love and it becomes the decisive measure of the work of love. This represents a momentous shift from what God does in and through the cross to what God does in and through the life of Jesus, which culminates in the cross. On this basis, Jesus was killed not by God but by the Romans, because of Jesus' passionate commitment to the work of love. This shows that the work of love is not empty religious rhetoric but divine action in the face of unjust structures embodied by the Roman Empire.

According to New Testament scholar Elisabeth Schussler Fiorenza, there are historical reasons for adopting this alternative interpretation of the cross. To begin, crucifixion was a Roman form of execution, which the Romans retained for slaves, bandits, prisoners of war and revolutionaries. It involved the systematic degradation of the victim, which included flogging, a slow death and no burial. Under Roman rule, Jesus proclaimed the imminent arrival of an alternative *kingdom*. Understandably, the Romans could have seen Jesus as some kind of revolutionary. While Jesus' life-changing and world-turning domain was grounded in love, it could have easily been perceived as a threat because it had religious, social and political implications. It is also no surprise then that the Romans referred to Jesus on the cross as "the king of the Jews", that is, here is a leader of an *alternative* kingdom.

To summarize: the theme of love is patently clear in the cruci-fixion, which is not a grisly story for the sake of a churlish god, but a love story for the sake of humanity. Jesus is killed by the Romans; not to gratify a wrathful God but because Jesus was radically committed to the way of love. Jesus put himself at risk. He chose the way of vulnerability, and others could not cope with it. In this light, the cross becomes the quintessential symbol of the horizon of love.

Everything considered, the life and teachings of Jesus are offered here as a touchstone for understanding love. In truth, we learn plenty about Jesus' understanding of love from: the gospels, his teachings about the kingdom, the banquet as event and symbol, and the meaning of the cross. Unquestionably, this love is magnanimous, joy-filled and inclusive. It is eminently practical. It is not an empty piety but a passionate work, which dares to challenge the status quo. It comes alive in action, as it responds to real people. Significantly, love has an affinity with those who are different, on the edge, and bear the stigma for being so. This final point bears repeating: the gracious acceptance of people who are different is not a marginal interest, but core business in the horizon of love.

A Life Lived Under the Horizon of Love

The horizon of love and the figure of Jesus work hand in hand. With its commitment to love, the life of Jesus has something to offer our understanding of the horizon of love. Equally, the love horizon finds its focus in the subversive Jesus. Thus, the love horizon provides the big picture so that we can get our bearings. In the process, the love horizon as background draws our attention to Jesus in the foreground.

For Jesus, an encounter with the mystery of the reign of God means that we are irresistibly swept up by, and into, this whirlwind of love. In the Jesus tradition, love creates community. In the Jesus tradition, love is a gift of divine encounter, but it is also cultivated as the highest of virtues. That's the genius of the Sermon on the Mount. What's more, the love of Jesus embodies a value commitment to the well-being of other people, which is expressed in extravagant acts of love. This is the horizon of love writ large. In this light, the meaning of the crucifixion is not found in a wrathful God demanding a scapegoat, but in an impassioned Jesus caught up in the power of love. This is a life lived inside the horizon of love.

It would be useful to draw out further the theological implications of this kind of thinking. First, the Jesus tradition presents an example of a life that is lived to the full, under the horizon of love. But you do not have to be a Christian or remotely religious to find in Jesus, as exemplar, an alternative way of living. Second, for a Christian, Jesus is an exemplar too. But in setting the example, there is also a compelling sense of Jesus as *icon* or *sacrament* of the mystery of the God of the quirky banquet. Jesus embodies and expresses something of the mystery. Call it spirit or divine chemistry? There is no priestly alchemy. On the contrary, there is something working in and through people who have been swept up by the power of love. Third, if God is love then love is God. Wherever there is love, whether it is romantic, familial, friendly or neighborly, there is a divine synergy that is more than the sum of the parts. I am not claiming, however, that a 21st century understanding of God can be reduced solely to human love; rather I am elevating the status of human love, on the premise that the divine comes to life and flourishes in love.

Unfortunately, life is convoluted. There is no Sunday school story, biblical reference or voice from heaven, which can provide simple step-by-step operating instructions for the dilemmas of the 21st century. Not at all. The old way of seeing God, which turns God into a *man* and places *him* among the clouds, gets in the way of us seeing and experiencing ourselves, others and the divine. Yes, this destructive split, this imposed division, this revered dualism between God and world is half the problem. Yet it is love that gives us a clue about another way of seeing the relationship between God and the world. It is our experience of love that gives us an insight into the mystery of God. So, rather than concentrate on outmoded stereotypes or caricatures of God, let's return to love.

Love means something of the divine is rekindled (incarnated) in the human heart, which gives us a new way of looking at ourselves, others and the world. Does this mean God is nothing more than a form of wish-fulfillment or a projection of human needs? Well partly, because if God works from the inside-out, then wish-fulfillment and projection, yearning and desire, are sacraments of divine presence *in the flesh*. They are signs of the spirit warming and illuminating our interior life.

This line of criticism of religion challenges the God-stereotypes, and I am in full agreement with that; but it also lends weight to a more vital, grounded and innate understanding of the divine. It is only after we have a glimmer of a God, who works from the inside out, that we are in a position to appreciate the concept of love I am offering and maybe, just maybe, to appreciate the Church's tradition in a new way.

When it comes to faith, I cannot answer the big questions in strictly scientific terms. There is always a leap of faith. It is not a leap, however, which abandons *all* semblance of reason. Actually, by construing the leap in terms of experience, love and relationships, it is a reasonable leap. By reasonable, however, I do not mean it is a soft touch or an easy option. This faith unzips us, as it outs love-substitutes, exposes sham and hypocrisy, and drags us kicking and screaming into unsafe places. But it does not achieve this from the outside, by the intervention of a god who is too good, too remote or too holy for love. So, if we are going to use the word *god*, then let it be a God who works from the inside out in the name of love, and not an interfering old man in the sky or a commodity for sale on-line. God is love and love is God. This is the divine glue which brings us and holds us together.

Finally, I am using the word *love* in a number of interrelated ways: as horizon, virtue and emotion. As horizon, love is the decisive perspective or frame that we bear in mind, which shapes our thinking about people and life's dilemmas. In Christianity,

Jesus signals and celebrates the love horizon as discovered in the quirky kingdom. Further, to work within the horizon of love is to develop love as a virtue. While there are variations in *the capacity* to love, *the disposition* to love can be fostered by dint of goodwill and habit. This is as much an expression of an expanded sense of self as it is a selfless act. This is precisely what Jesus tried to model to his disciples. Ironically, it is often the people on the margins who see and understand this. Furthermore, as emotion, love in action can never be a neutral exercise. It is not separate from virtue. On the contrary, emotions involve value-judgments. For example, we love lovers, friends or family members because we value them and value their love. In Christianity, Jesus places a premium on the value of people. As a result, he makes judgments in the name of love, for love is the decisive measure. Only love matters. Rules, regulations and principles come second, and then if and only if, they manage to pass the test of love. So, in the spirit of the unconventional kingdom, we intentionally cultivate both a personal disposition and a social environment, where life's dilemmas are seriously addressed by taking people seriously. This entails us acknowledging and embracing difference, by seeing and understanding people with the eyes of love. All this is the work of love; so that making love in real life is the *true* vocation of everyone who embraces the quirky kingdom.

I am celebrating the theme of love, which is the decisive and defining measure of all things Christian. But it is subversive. It begins with our perceptions: we see others differently, we act differently and we are transformed in the process. This love is a broker of change, but the changes are not cosmetic. They penetrate deeply into human lives and institutions. So, while inherently non-violent, it is ultimately life changing and world turning. As a result, it is not for the timid, because it changes us. This is love upside down. Recall our lurid fascination with the love-substitutes of our day? When people are captive to superficial or counterfeit forms of love, they have nothing to do with others who are different. In contrast, the key characteristic of the love horizon is the way we see others, especially those who are different, because love begins when we look at others as irreplaceable. With this love, instead of ignoring or persecuting others who are different, we embrace them. But it begins with our perceptions, our attitude and our willingness to be open.

Recall the game of spin the bottle? I had seen Sally many times, but suddenly I saw her differently. Once we see people this way, the other characteristics of love emerge and flourish. Such love is inclusive and magnanimous. We accept people. We invite them into our lives as they are, just as they accept and delight in us. There is a new generosity of spirit that wants the best for them and they bring out the new in us.

The cutting edge for the horizon of love comes from re-visiting Christianity. Specifically, we have new eyes. Jesus is no longer meek and mild, but rather a subversive prophet of justice and wisdom teacher of love. The reign of God is of great importance in the development of the horizon of love. It is a quirky and disruptive kingdom; turning the world up the right way. While it is not a physical entity, it has practical outcomes. Above all, it changes who we are and the world we live in. But the real test is how love addresses real life.

4

RESPONSE TO DIFFERENCE

If I am walking down the street and I happen to see an obese man coming the other way, I scarcely notice him. If an obese woman is coming the other way, however, I often feel a sarcastic remark welling up in me, trying to come to the surface, only to poison the air. While I would never say anything offensive, I think it. This means I am not taking her seriously as a person of innate value; I have not seen her. I saw an obese woman; I did not see the person.

It also means I am kidding myself too, if I think I am immune to the ways of men. The great myth of middle class educated men is that we have dealt with these issues, that is, we read a book or joined a men's group and now our humanity is neat and tidy. But from Afghanistan to Zimbabwe, from A to Z, violence is a way of life and it is related to how we respond to difference. Women are different from men and I am interested in the nature of men's response to this difference. How does love change this? What hope is there for change?

The Little Girl who Lived under the Bed

Madeline was a little girl who lived under her bed. She would start the night by climbing into her bed in the customary manner and then she would go to ground as soon as the lights went out. It was her bunker, because Dad could not stoop down and hit her there. So when he was on the warpath, cursing, staggering and punching, she would be safely ensconced under the bed with pillow, blanket and a worn-out teddy bear. But it was more than a bunker. It was a sanctuary where spirit and imagination were nourished. Madeline played games too, real and make-believe, which fed her soul. In her mind's eye, Madeline created new memories as she traveled to beautiful places and encountered many kind people. But she never forgot the terror.

Madeline was 9 years of age and the youngest of 4 children. She worked hard at school. She also attended Sunday school at the local church and she loved it. This was extraordinary, considering her family thought that the Church was a complete waste of time. Despite her family's skepticism, Madeline saved her weekly allowance in order to secure a small gold cross. In monetary terms the cross was worth very little, but she wore it on a matching chain with pride, because it was a symbol of the possibility of another life.

Unfortunately, Madeline's home was ruled by hostility as her father was a violent alcoholic. Her mother, a frequent victim of alcohol-fuelled rage, was compliant. She exacerbated the situation by making lame excuses for him like "the war changed him" or "his home life was terrible". Like a dead possum in the chimney, the house reeked of fear and betrayal.

Mom had given up on life long ago. She was a strange brew. In the same breath, she could be subservient to Dad, charming with friends and cruel to her children. When the children were small, she was a good mother. But things changed. As they got older, she abused them more and more by withholding affection and approval. She repeatedly held the promise of love in front of them, like a carrot, and then withdrew it at the last moment with a disingenuous smile. She was an accomplice, but Dad was the perpetrator.

While Madeline's story bears witness to the universal impact of the violence of men, I am not about to launch a vitriolic attack on men. To state the obvious: there are many men who are good, decent and compassionate. Nevertheless, I am conscious that when we try and balance the ledger like this, by pointing out the good men, we run the risk of losing a sense of clarity and urgency about the plight of Madeline and her *sisters*; for there are many others like her in the world. Clearly, we need to address the issues of difference and vulnerability: asking why some men behave so badly and what it is about love that offers hope. But first, let's turn to a contemporary puzzle.

For centuries, men have been singing the praises of women. For the sake of women, men have been slaying dragons, fighting Vikings, scaling mountains, crossing oceans, writing poems and penning love songs. In the name of love, men have been willing to surrender wealth, sever limbs and offer their lives. It is exhausting. Of course, the motivation has been mixed. There have been signs of the presence of testosterone, as well as altruism, in all these daring deeds. Sometimes it is sincere, but misplaced valor. Sometimes it is a ploy to get a woman into bed. Other times it is a way of establishing who the top dog is. Specifically, the latter are primal displays of strength, which are more for the sake of discouraging competitors than wooing lovers. Today some men in order to impress use charm, wit and learning instead of drawn swords. For example, there is the dreaded wine buff. Worse still, there's the nightmare scenario of two wine buffs jousting over the one damsel at the same dinner party. It is a slightly more elevated form of two snorting bulls in a paddock.

In the end, while this manly chorus of praise for women resounds around the world, something is not right. On the one hand, there is this chorus, which may be well-intended, but it is often fanciful. On the other hand, there is a grim-faced litany of violence, which is well documented and largely ignored. This litany includes domestic violence, date rape, sexual assault, sexual harassment, sexual abuse, child brides, sex slaves, female genital mutilation, systemic rape in war and the murder of women accused of adultery (who are executed in the name of honor). So Madeline is no orphan; she has many sisters. What makes many of us angry is that their plight is trivialized or ignored because it happens to *a handful* of women *over there*. In the horizon of love, these are our sisters. Like Madeline, they all deserve to be safe. They all deserve to be loved. At the least, they all deserve an honest explanation. Where to now? While there is no single explanation, how we deal with difference is a major factor. In particular, why is it that some men have major problems with gender difference?

Difference

Love is a personal response to others as persons, which engages heart and will, so that we see others and our relationships in a new light. It is about responding to people in real life situations. All this involves us making decisions; that is, we choose to move out into the world in the name and spirit of love, or we retreat from the world. Love, then, is not a theory but a practice, which is embodied by persons in relationships, in circles of trusted and valued others. It is our vulnerability as ordinary human beings, which ensures love remains present and does not evaporate or ossify. It is vulnerability that keeps us open, receptive and transparent. It is the acceptance of vulnerability, which enables us both to honor difference and to create community so that love may flourish.

But all is not plain sailing; there are problems. The French Jewish philosopher Jacques Derrida points out the dangers of community. Firstly, the word *communion* can mean common office, functions or duties. In the best sense of the word then, a community is about a shared life. This is its strength. Second, the word *communion* can also be interpreted in terms of common defenses or fortifications. If love is gone, and a willingness to be open has dissipated, then a community can develop an impenetrable boundary. This is its weakness. This is a sobering reminder that the presence of love, expressed in and through a community, does not in any way mean moral perfection or superiority. Love is a gift. But it can depart. It is also important to bear in mind that the idea and the reality of *community* is a two-edged sword. Positively a community, in the name of love, facilitates the development of relationships in an inclusive manner, where people are valued regardless of differences. In fact, differences are honored. Negatively a community, in the name of vested interests, fosters the development of relationships in an exclusive manner; just like the Christmas caprice where the family made it clear, by silence, whispers and neglect, that Adrian and Janet were unacceptable because they were different. Without a doubt, how we respond to difference is critical.

I am curious about what it is that makes some men violent toward women. I suspect it has to do with the nature of difference and how we respond to it. As well as sexism, the issue of difference emerges in many areas like racism. Croatian theologian Miroslav Volf has done a lot of work on difference. His thinking has been shaped by the conflict that took place in the former Yugoslavia (1991-1995). He asserts, "It may not be too much to claim that the future of our world will depend on how we deal with identity and difference". So difference is a big issue, but what is the nature of difference and why is it important? With racism, obvious examples come to mind like segregation, apartheid or ethnic cleansing. But racism is often below the radar; flying beneath our defenses. Sometimes it surfaces as *reverse* racism. For instance, years ago, I remember a multi-faith memorial service for the London bombings. A young Imam participated in the service and shared in refreshments afterwards. He impressed everyone with his goodwill and courtesy. What struck me as odd was the inordinate fuss we made over the fact that he was *a nice person*, as if he would behave otherwise. There's also what I call *selective* racism. In Australia, we constantly sing the praises of the thousands of immigrants who, over the decades, have contributed so much to our country and culture. But when it comes to talking about indigenous Australians, the aboriginals and Torres Strait Islanders, our response is often muted and sometimes malevolent. Now, what has this got to do with women?

Racism and sexism have the issue of *difference* in common, and studies in racism can illuminate the problems we have with difference, but it seems easier to talk more openly about racism than sexism. There is still a sense of racism being *over there, somewhere else* or *somebody else's problem*, which is ludicrous in a multi-cultural country like America, Australia or the United Kingdom. Of course, I would reject this out of hand because, in the horizon of love, people of a different race who are *over there* are still my sisters and brothers. With sexism, and the women of our lives, we are more often than not talking about actual mothers, sisters, partners, daughters and friends. It is too close for comfort. For instance, I find it easier to talk academically about the long journey women have had to make, in terms of the vote, admission to universities and the glass ceiling, than why I occasionally feel vulnerable in the presence of women, especially my wife. Actual relationships elicit real fears.

The sticking point is: how do we deal with difference and why is it so hard to name it as a problem in the first place? As an example, it is worth having a look at the issue of blood. In some cultures, blood is a symbol of life, but a woman's blood is often a symbol of shame. Even today, it is only in recent times that we have dared to utter the word *menstruation* in public. Prior to this, it was a nod, a wink or a euphemism like "It's the time of the month". In ancient Jewish-Christian religious settings, blood was a symbol of defilement. For example, menstrual blood was considered as the archetype of impurity. A menstruating woman was considered ill. The birth of a child meant that the mother had to undergo a period of blood purification, which was longer if the baby was female. This was worked out in a sacrificial context; that is, there was a sense in which women were scapegoats for maintaining the ritual purity that underpinned the sacrificial system.

Women are different from men, and unfortunately this presses all the male buttons. But women pay the price for this; emotionally, physically and spiritually. This is perverse in the light of what we know about the human body and the wonder of birth. Moreover, what kind of religion is it, when its ritual purity is demanding and damning of women? So how do we move from fearing to embracing difference? Surely, things have improved since then.

Long before I played spin the bottle with Sally, I suspected girls were not the same as boys. Not surprisingly, I have also come to realize that women are different from men. In the West, historically and culturally, we have struggled with difference. For instance the tension in courtly love of the middle Ages and romantic works of the 19th century plays on the theme of difference. Apparently, compared to pillaging Vikings, women are treated better in courtly love, Shakespeare and 19th romanticism. But none of this sits well. It is a veneer. We know for example of the double standards of many a 19th century gentleman. So, what's the stumbling block? Women repeatedly pay the price for men's inability to deal with vulnerability. In so doing, women are harmed and men diminish or destroy the possibility of a life enriched by love. Therefore, it is important that we explore more deeply real vulnerability.

The Heart of Vulnerability

Let me draw together some of the earlier themes relating to the question of vulnerability, which is the elephant in the sitting room. Previously, I observed that vulnerability is *the latest thing*. Clearly, we know the sales shtick: if we are not willing to be vulnerable, then we will not value the journey. The problem with the popular view is that it is a cheap version of vulnerability. In real-life, vulnerability is costly because we are dragged in kicking and screaming. As a result, our response is less "This'll be good for me" and more "What the hell is going on?" This is what it means to be vulnerable. In other words, the popular view fails to grasp the depth of suffering, which underscores the experience of vulnerability. This is the kind of suffering that burns heart and soul. This is *affliction*. What's more, the popular version does not build community. At best, it is a glimpse of an unreachable utopia. It creates expectations that cannot be fulfilled.

I realize, however, I am at risk of being too general. So let's have a look into the heart of vulnerability as it relates to men, because there is something about how some men handle vulnerability that is directly related to the abuse of women.

It is three in the morning and I have been pacing the hallway for an hour. I am feeling as sick as a dog with worry. Our 15 year old son has gone to a party. After protracted negotiations, where I conceded a lot of ground, we agreed that he would be home by one. At five minutes passed one, I began to clock-watch. I started reassuring myself that he was a trustworthy young person and that he had to learn how to deal with this. Inevitably, I began tossing and turning, when my wife said tenderly "Go to the spare room". So, taking her advice, I got out of bed and entered the hallway of anguish.

So, here I am, pacing up and down. The tension is unbearable. I know he is a responsible young man, and if there is anything wrong, then he will call me on his cell phone. Even so, I am beside myself. All semblance of sanity has gone as I shriek "I can't take this anymore". He is in trouble. Yes, there has been a fight. Gate crashers have barged into the party causing a violent fracas. Worse still, he has been in a terrible car crash. That's it. He cannot call because he is lying on the road, facedown in a pool of blood; if only I had told him earlier how much I loved him. But hang on, what if it's drugs? I bet the police are arriving at the party right now, making arrests and ringing parents; and so I begin to rehearse "Not my son officer".

As I move from fretting to wailing, the front door squeaks. I race back into our bedroom, pirouette, re-entering the hallway, stretching and yawning as though I'd just woken up. Half way down the hall he greets me with "How come you're up?" I reply meekly, resisting the temptation to hug him and check for broken limbs, "I'm getting a glass of water". I sound pathetic. He rolls his eyes in disgust, says good night and goes to bed. He is sound asleep in less than a minute, while I am still in the hallway, bewildered and fixed to the spot. That's vulnerability. It is not cute or cuddly. It is a black hole, threatening to consume us. This is what it means to be unzipped.

For most of us, there is something about difference that elicits the feeling of vulnerability. For many men, there is something about women, which elicits this vulnerability. What does this look like? The preceding interaction is a good example. In that instance, my son is unable or unwilling to acknowledge my angst and I am unable to transcend my fear. Maybe it is similar for mothers and daughters. I cannot say. But for me, this is a classic male interaction. I do not mean by this that we are all weak and wretched, but rather, when we are stripped bare and there is nothing we can do; there is a hit-or-miss quality to our relating. While this is not true of all my male relationships, it is true of many. In this instance, my son and I were literally at cross-purposes: practically and emotionally. Looking back, my biggest problem was not admitting to myself "I am anxious and there's nothing I can do". This comes close to the heart of the meaning of being unzipped. Like waiting up late for a teenager, difference has the capacity to make us feel apprehensive and powerless. Significantly, I do not like myself when I am unzipped.

What is the point of this, especially in relation to the work of love? Let's explore a little further the male response to vulnerability, because this bears a great deal on men's response to women. In the case of Madeline's father, while there are biographical explanations and extenuating circumstances, his treatment of Madeline expresses something of both his negative attitude toward women and his inability to cope with his own interior life. He is a man out of control. Significantly, violence or abuse is bound to happen when damaged people, like Madeline's father, fail to take responsibility for their own vulnerability.

Now, let's take a punt and explore further the attitude of men toward women, without condemning all men but with a searing honesty that befits the courage of love. To be perfectly honest, men are funny things as women have the capacity to disarm us completely. Sure, we are good at slaying dragons and writing love songs, but we struggle with what it means to be human, that is a sexual, spiritual, emotional human being. Certainly there are powerful evolutionary drives at work that are part of the problem, like the primal need to keep the herd flourishing, but there is also vulnerability symbolized by the male appendage. Ah yes, the not so humble penis.

While I am not going to be gratuitous, we need to be honest because there is something pitiable, even tragic, about the significance that is attributed by men to the offending appendage, so that size becomes *the* measure of the man. It is a fact of life that it matters to many men, whether it is the size of the appendage, the car or the salary. It is the engine that drives our herding, crusading and conquering. It is also a reminder of the presence of a lurking sense of inadequacy. Unzipped again. And I thought I had *mastered* life. But there are big questions here: like what does it mean to be a man? Why is it hard to talk about this without making jokes, using gallows humor or declaring repeatedly just how much we like football and hunting? Above all, how do heterosexual men relate to others? They are big questions because, in the heart of man, the primal drive and a debilitating angst are twinned. Without the drive, there would be fewer achievements. But it is the angst, the pull of the black hole, which undermines much of the achievement. All this, however, is not a matter of idle theories or airy abstractions.

I have done the lot from therapy, self-help books to hugging my male friends, but to be honest, at times it feels funny to be a man. What does it all mean? Even now, I run the risk of ridicule, but I am not complaining; I just haven't figured it out. Maybe that's the problem: that being male is not something we solve, as it is part of the human condition that we learn to live with. It is about being comfortable in our own skins. Historically, we see the signs of men wrestling with, or retreating from, this lurking sense of inadequacy with Origen's self-castration, Augustine's checkered past, Henry VIII's treatment of women and the private lives of philandering prime ministers and presidents. We have done all sorts of crazy things, including blaming women, beginning with Eve and the Garden of Eden. In the so-called story of the Fall, Eve becomes the fall-girl, while Adam stands there idle. In due course, we got stuck into the hags, the witches, little sisters, mothers-in-law, old women, ugly women and fat women. We made scapegoats of women, at the same time as we praised them in song.

Let me reiterate: this is not about bashing men. But if there is one thing I have learnt from the Jesus tradition, then it is that honest engagement with others is an integral part of the character of love. It is the price of love. It is human to be unzipped. It is human to feel powerless; and this is the kind of humanity that the subversive Jesus addresses and embraces. So, what is the nature of love's work?

Love's Work

The causes of Madeline's father's violence are legion. It is likely that his genes, temperament, upbringing, war-time experience and alcoholism conspired against him, his family and Madeline. While mom did not help, he was the violent one and the family was vulnerable. In spite of countless apologies, acts of contrition and promises to reform, he was the one who terrorized Madeline. In spite of his own frailty, he was morally responsible for the well-being and safety of his family. Now there are many issues here, but the primary issue is violence toward women and men's response to difference, which can lead to violence. Sadly, Madeline is no orphan. So, how do we address this?

We address our existential dilemmas and moral quandaries from within a particular horizon or framework and I am putting forward the horizon of love. I am not saying that love, as the horizon, will establish straightforward, unambiguous moral solutions. For example, the significance of killing or murder varies enormously, depending on circumstances, intention and consequences (war, whaling, euthanasia, abortion, home break-in). I am arguing, however, that love as the context for living and ethical decision making, changes the way we see, understand and approach the whole thing. So what's the issue with Madeline?

In Christianity, the life and example of Jesus embodies an urgent call to a passionate commitment to the work of love and signals a renewed hope in the spirit of love, working through people of goodwill. Without a doubt, love is *the* most important aspect of the quirky kingdom. It is *the* horizon or frame of reference for seeing, judging and living. This means that within the horizon of love we are compelled to take an active and personal interest in Madeline. What's more, while love does not provide a list of moral answers for all of life's vexing questions, it does spell out an unambiguous moral imperative for personal engagement. By personal, I mean we get involved. We cannot run away from the situation and hide behind pious platitudes, academic abstractions or armchair solutions. This active engagement, however, does not rule out the need for exercising a degree of discernment in assessing Madeline's situation. This is what the ancients called *wisdom*, which is always grounded in reflection upon human experience. There is no genuine discernment, however, without genuine engagement. In the final analysis, love calls us to choose Madeline's side. If we look at her as a person under the horizon of love, if we see her for the first time, then we are led inescapably to the conclusion that the situation is totally unacceptable. It is not on. Madeline is a real person, the abuse is real and this situation is very much love's domain. Above all, love cannot turn a blind eye to the suffering of Madeline. Critically, the decision to side with Madeline is a corollary of Jesus' subversive understanding of love. This is love upside down.

Let's recall that love was indispensible to the ministry of Jesus and his movement. Love God and your neighbor as yourself: it is as simple as that. This is not love as an abstract universal principle, but rather it is love as a concrete response by Jesus to real people on the edge of society. It is important to note the significance of these people, being *on the edge*, to appreciate the character of Christian love. These people are different, and as a result they are alienated. The different, the other and the unacceptable, pay a price for their estrangement in spiritual, social and economic terms. In the first century, they pay a price at two levels: the pain and the stigma.

At a moral level, the sick bear an extra load, because the cause of illness was attributed to the sin of the ill person or their parents. At a social level, they bear the shame for being different. They are stigmatized. There is no place of honor for them. This is *affliction*. This makes Jesus' unflinching commitment to love all the more radical.

The emotive power of the story of the woman who hemorrhaged, which is an example of this kind of commitment, derives as much from the courage of the woman as it does the compassion of Jesus (Matthew 9:20-22). In an ancient agrarian community, the woman who had been hemorrhaging for twelve years is different and inferior by virtue of gender. But she also suffers the stigma, that is, the emotional, social and religious consequences, because she is hemorrhaging. She is unclean. With great courage, she breaks the rules and touches Jesus' garment.

He responds with "Take heart, daughter, your faith has made you well". His response is an extraordinary amalgam of respect for the woman, blessing on her life and the re-inclusion of a "daughter" back into community. This is the work of love.

The editor of this story, conscious of the radical nature of Jesus' act of love, places the story within another story, which is the healing of Jairus' daughter. Jairus is a leader in the synagogue, who as a *gatekeeper* keeps hemorrhaging women and the like out of community. What an irony: Jairus must wait until the hemorrhaging woman has been healed by Jesus before his own daughter can be attended to. In the social world of the quirky kingdom, it is downside up.

From Mary Magdalene, Francis of Assisi, Florence Nightingale to Martin Luther King, the lives of our luminaries have been characterized by a generosity of spirit. In the lives of the lesser lights, there too have been generous and courageous acts of love. Such love is realized in relation to others who are different by dint of poverty, class, race or gender. Difference evokes, like a catalyst, big-hearted acts of love; that is, we need the other in order to realize our full humanity. Unintentionally, we sometimes patronize others, when others in fact bring out the best in us. So I am extending an invitation to look at Madeline, to see and understand her, and to take up the shared work of love.

In the past, men have been fighting Vikings and scaling mountains, all in the name of love. In the present, we need a new, more authentic kind of heroism. The new heroism has two aspects. It is about befriending ourselves and others by facing vulnerability and living creatively with difference. It is about naming violence and injustice and working together to change it. This means that if we live under the horizon of love, then the work of love is not a chore, but a shared vocation for women and men of good faith. It is a shared calling to go beyond personal limits and self-interest, in the name of love.

In my own situation, I know many ordinary men who are

speaking about their vulnerability with a candor that was unheard of in previous generations. Their world has been turned upside down. It is a good thing that men are reading books and attending courses on what it means to be a man. What's more, over the years I have worked with a number of female priests. On several occasions, I have had male colleagues come to me and say, without a hint of condescension, "I was uncomfortable working with her at first, until I came to know and love her". This sounds so obvious, so painfully obvious. How come they could not see this earlier? But it is only obvious from within the horizon of love.

In truth, there is a terrible litany of violence against countless, often invisible women. As a consequence, some women have understandably lost all trust in men; a trust which may never be restored. So, there are no easy answers here. But this only serves to underline the importance of all of us getting on with the work of love. Difference and how we deal with it is central to the work of love. Love, however, can transform us so that we bravely do the work of love for Madeline and all her sisters, by seeing women for the first time, hearing their stories and working with them in love.

We need more than this, however, because we are talking about the need for substantial cultural change. There are major social justice issues that need to be addressed and only a love that dares to turn the world upside down, can give us cause for hope. But all this begins with a personal transformation, which is immersed in the life of the quirky kingdom. Indeed, there is something profound about the relationship between the personal impact of the spiritual and the possibility of broader social change. So while there are many possible approaches to all these issues, which are based on love, mine is specifically grounded in the ministry of Jesus and all our sisters and brothers who have the courage to love. This courage risks everything, even death.

5

DRAWN TO THE SEA

Care for the environment is a critical issue, but some days it all seems too much like hard work. I find myself thinking gloomily, "If our governments struggle to work effectively on the ecological crisis, how can I do anything?" Call it eco-overkill, but on those days, the distance between me and the environment is unbridgeable. Nevertheless, I cannot let it go. There are powerful green memories, which have permanently shaped me. So, like many others, I have not surrendered the hope that dares to believe that maybe, just maybe, love is our best chance for the redemption of the earth. But there are some tough questions that have to be addressed. What are these *green memories* and why are they important? Can we talk about loving the environment? What difference would love make anyway?

A Night at the Prom

The Prom refers to Wilson's Promontory, which is on the south coast of Australia; it is not a school or college debutante's ball. It is a superb national park with magnificent eucalyptus forests, imposing rock formations and beautiful beaches, all bounded by the sea. When I was 17, I spent several days there on a hiking expedition with friends. I was going through a serious phase; writing poetry, drinking cheap red wine and reading very serious authors.

One magic evening, a violent storm descended upon the

Prom. The elements had conspired against me, or perhaps on my behalf, making it impossible to sleep. So I got up and entered the night. On leaving the tent, I started to walk then canter toward nearby cliffs, as this was the best place to enjoy a good storm. The cliffs were about 200 feet in height, with a commanding view of the ocean. On arriving I sat on the edge of the cliff, with my feet dangling over, resting against the cliff face. Up above, the lightning was busy, but it was the sound of the rolling thunder that attracted my attention. There was something spellbinding about the tone, the sheer depth of sound, as each reverberation sagely proclaimed "nothing else matters". Inexorably, however, I was drawn to the sea.

I sat perched on the cliff top for hours. Occasionally I looked up and around, but I constantly found my gaze returning toward the mesmerizing sea. I felt a sense of both exhilaration and calm. What's more, this space, this mood, this serenity returns to me even now in the worst of moments. So I have clung on to and been fed by this memory. In my imagination I go there regularly. I am renewed every time the moment is re-lived. So, while it is hard to explain, there is something about the environment that is life giving: spiritually as well as physically. But oh how quickly we forget these sacred moments. So, I need to say a little more about the sea.

Contrary to popular opinion, we do not have kangaroos bounding up and down the main streets of Australian cities. But we have beaches, fabulous beaches and a never-ending coastline. Unsurprisingly, the spiritual life of most Australians is implicitly immersed in and bounded by the sea. We love swimming, surfing, sailing, fishing, walking and living by the sea. So we cling to the water's edge. But what has this got to do with love? It has to do with how the environment engages us and draws something out of us. It is also about how our memories of engagement shape our lives.

I have green memories. More precisely, I have blue memories.

Like sacraments, memories of the sea draw me out of myself and into the world. The sea is my leading metaphor for the spiritual life. When I pray, I am contemplating the ebbing and flowing of life or spirit. This is why our home is filled with paintings of the sea. In fact, the sea, the sky and the earth are primal symbols, which occur universally in many cultures and religions, expressing humankind's deep affinity with the environment.

If love, however, has to do with a mutual sense of delight in others then we cannot love the sea, let alone a polar bear, in the same way as we love another human being, as it will hardly be reciprocated. In this regard, the environment does not fit snugly into my approach to love. But the night at the Prom reminds me that somehow, someway, I am connected to the sea, the earth and the sky. Instinctively I feel we are part of the same horizon of love. What's more, because I love others and I am loved by others, I am morally obliged to encompass the environment in my dreaming, my thinking and my actions. If the environment is critically damaged, then so are my friends and their children's children. It would be a shallow and bloodless love that did not include the earthly life of real people.

More importantly, while I cannot have an encounter with a polar bear, like the one I did with Sally; love makes a difference to my attitude toward the earth and its creatures. So my focus is not on, for example, facts and figures about climate change, but rather it is directed toward our attitude and behavior in relation to the environment. On that basis, I am very much interested in our *personal* response to the world. So where and how do we begin to make this personal link? Without a doubt, the problem of excess is a major contributor to environmental problems. This is true in both corporate and personal domains. Extravagantly expensive suits like mine, and other love-substitutes, are classic symbols of excess and what excess represents, which is fundamentally a lack of love for the self, the other and the world. So, let's think more about excess.

Nothing Exceeds like Excess

I remember the pie nights of my youth, which occurred on a regular basis at the local football club. Now, the meat pie may be the single greatest culinary creation ever to come out of Australia. While I suspect crude prototypes of the pie first came out from England in convict ships, Australians have perfected and exalted the humble pie. Almost by osmosis, however, the lowly sausage roll was also developed, though it failed to achieve the same standing as the pie. The recipe for the sausage roll is complicated. In essence, the sausage roll is mince meat wrapped in pastry and baked in the oven. Brilliant. In my view, the sausage roll was the gastronomic highlight of the pie night.

The pie night was held in an old hall with wooden trestles in the middle. Roughly hewn pine tabletops, sitting precariously on top of the trestles, were covered with tablecloths and laden with pies, sausage rolls, white bread and paper serviettes. Only the mothers used the serviettes. As teenagers we waited impatiently for our coach, the notorious Joffa Jackson, to give the signal to commence eating. But he was not the main problem. There was a large muscular boy called Bruce. He was the archetypal bully, who had all the charm and grace of Vlad the Impaler. Predictably, when the signal was given he moved in with the force and effect of a bulldozer. Singlehandedly, Bruce tried to eat all the sausage rolls.

This is not the time or place for a political diatribe. But from the beginning of the slave trade to the present day, nations and corporations have tried to consume all the sausage rolls. Of course, the source of justification for this demand has shifted from claims made on the basis of absolute power to so-called deference to the demands of shareholders. But it is not just the wheelers and dealers who have capitulated to this orgy of excess. Expensive suits are testimony to the obstinate fact that a lot of us, including me, want a piece of the action. We want to be in. These are telling measures of the hole within and the fear of being unzipped. Take off our new suits, and take away the bling, and we are all left standing buck naked.

So, the success of excess says two things: we do not respect ourselves or the environment. In terms of the environment, we have been raised to think that the wilderness is dangerously different. It is a primal threat, harboring all sorts of demons, which years later are projected (or pixilated) on to our screens in the form of King Kong or Godzilla. There is a burgeoning industry, which is devoted to finding new ways of personifying that sense of threat. This is reinforced by some crowd favorites: so beware of the great white shark, snakes, crocodiles and polar bears.

If it is a threat, then it needs to be tamed. Remove the threats, clear the trees, dry up the wetlands and fence it all in. Unfortunately, elements of the Christian tradition have been used to justify this conquest tradition, like the first of the two biblical creation stories, "Fill the earth and subdue it; and have dominion over the fish of the sea and over the birds of the air and over every living thing that moves upon the face of the earth". In reality, while this is a mythological story, it has been used with deadly effect. Tragically, we have fallen out of love with the world. Our memories are short lived; for we have forgotten the deep links we have with the sea, the earth and the sky, and all living creatures that are part of the horizon of love.

The Last Polar Bear

But let's try and ground our ecological reflection. Imagine a majestic polar bear swimming in the Arctic Ocean, but at serious risk of drowning. Unthinkable. Such an image has been on our television screens of late. It is a haunting image, because this creature is about to go under. It is a damning image too, as the ice is melting at an alarming rate. The bottom line is that polar bears, who are fantastic swimmers, have to rest. The reduction of ice-flows means there are fewer places to rest. As a species, they may die out. This lone vulnerable polar bear is a powerful symbol of the current ecological crisis. While I am a climate change believer, there are skeptics. But the idea of the polar bear, the creature and the metaphor, still holds true, as it draws our attention to a surfeit of environmental concerns ranging from pollution, reduced bio-diversity, de-forestation and the loss of top soil to diminishing natural resources.

It is fair to say that the environment is under a serious far-reaching, long-term threat. So, what about our response? It disturbs me, but that is not quite right. It also has something to do with sorrow. It is like the death of a friend and every time I see the image of another ecological casualty, a wave of grief washes over me. This is why there are days when it all seems too much like hard work. But more importantly, I am flagging links, our primal links with the world and its creatures. Remember the sea; remember the night at the Prom. This is about love and while it is not the same kind of love as shared human love, it is love nevertheless.

The polar bear, this wonderful loner of the north, is an icon for the global lament we need to have. Now, a lament is a passionate expression of grief, often articulated in ritual, song or verse. Without a shared lament, communities get stuck, stuck in depression or denial. In our societies, people are depressed by the immensity of the ecological destruction, the collateral damage of human excess. Before we can share in this lament, we need ritual or some kind a funeral. This is the funeral we have to have, which recognizes, honors and farewells the death of part of the environment. But why do we need a funeral?

If dear old Aunt Dorothy dies, do we carry on with business as usual? No. We weep in solitude and gather as friends and families to share our sorrow. Eventually, we know its time to say goodbye and we want to say it with grace and dignity, befitting the life and memory of Dorothy. Together as one, overcoming family differences or putting them aside, we gather to bid farewell. Symbols and eulogies bring her memory to life, while words and song bring our feelings to the surface. The coffin is sprinkled with holy water and the tears of all who loved her. In silence, six family members place the coffin on their shoulders. The crucifer moves forward, leading the procession and then, with a dozen pipers playing *Highland Cathedral*, the pipe organ kicks in. Not a dry eye in the house.

I suspect we need a global funeral rite for the death of the environment, at least in its *pristine* state. So I am with the pragmatists here, as we cannot go back and restore the world to what it was a thousand years ago, let alone a hundred. But I am with the lovers and the dreamers too, who feel a deep connection with the world and long to protect, preserve and renew what remains. It is time to love the world: openly and courageously. This too is a sign of the quirky kingdom.

A Green Jesus?

The love of God, as expressed in the Jesus movement, was characterized by a deep and expansive respect for all life. It was also typical of Jesus to proclaim his radical message of love through parables about the land and its creatures. This had roots in the Jewish prophetic tradition, which was acutely aware that humankind had an important link with the land. Obviously, these stories emerged from the life of an agrarian society. Nonetheless, while many were farmers and fishers, this was not taken as license for unrestrained use of ecological resources. There were checks and balances. The Sabbath year, for example, meant every seventh year the land was fallow, and there was also remission of debts. The Sabbath year served as a reminder that the people did not own the land. They were stewards, not owners of the created order.

In the first century, in particular, we find Jesus proclaiming the present and future impact of divine love in the language of the quirky kingdom. The quirky kingdom is concerned with the divine transformation that is taking place now and in the future, which turns the world upside down. But how, if at all, is this linked with the environment? While it is not true to describe Jesus as a modern environmentalist, he did have a deep affinity with the land by virtue of his birthright, upbringing and culture. Jesus was Jewish. He was brought up in an agrarian community, which had a lasting respect for the land and the poor. In Jewish thinking, if the poor are starving then the land suffers too and as a result, the religious practices of the day are deemed worthless. So it is prophets over profits, justice over excess and love over law. This was also premised on the idea of God as creator, which was expressed in the two creation mythologies in Genesis 1-3. Thus, in the thinking of Jesus there was an intimate link between God, the people and the land, such that the leaders of the ancient community were expected to care for both the land and the poor.

The idea that humankind has a special relationship with the environment is an integral part of the cultural and spiritual background of Jesus. This rich background is actively taken up and explored in the Jesus tradition, where nature and our dependence on nature are prophetic symbols of the quirky banquet. In the sayings and stories of Jesus, note the prevalence and interplay between images of farmers sowing and seed, seed and soil, grain and harvest, bearing fruit, bread and leaven, bread of life, living water, sea, fish and fishers, fishers of people, shepherds and sheep, the good shepherd, vines and vineyards, fruit of the vine, old wine and new wine. In other words, an innate sense of respect for the environment shapes the life of Jesus, and Jesus in turn gives shape and color to the life of the quirky kingdom through his provocative use of images of life on the land and by the sea. Implicitly and explicitly, love is the big issue here.

The love of the quirky kingdom means we are responsible to each other, for each other. We are also entrusted with the care of the earth; besides we cannot afford to eat all the sausage rolls. This moral demand cuts through the economic and political double speak of our time, which talks about striking a balance between environmental care and economic prudence, as if they were opposites. This rhetoric is usually laced with in-built threats: "If we care too much for the environment, we'll lose all our jobs". The inference is that the task of finding a balance between human needs and ecological sustainability is at best a nuisance and at worst an unattainable ideal.

All this rests on the assumption that the environment, in all its mystery and complexity, is an endless and expendable human resource. But it is not unlimited. It is not exclusively a human resource. Its meaning cannot be reduced to an expendable object. What's more, it demands something of us. Yes, it is not the time for empty rhetoric, superficial changes or token gestures. Our world needs to be inverted. So that care for the environment is no longer somebody else's problem. It is our problem. It is also our pleasure.

The environment has intrinsic worth because God saw that it was good and we are responsible for its care, hence the Sabbath year. So, I am not advocating that we necessarily go hugging trees, but maybe we can go, see and experience an old growth forest. Yes, let's look at the trees and see them for the first time. Let's experience that innate sense of ourselves and our world being encompassed by the horizon of love. Perhaps then we would return to daily life with a new sense of wonder and collective responsibility, so that the issue of *balance* is no longer a chore but a challenge; not a burden but a shared human vocation that we pursue together with passion and hope.

One day, my wife Anne and I were on an immense ocean beach. Coincidentally, its name was Discovery Bay. From memory the beach is sixty miles in length and on that day, we could not see a soul. We sat together in silence as we watched these wonderful waves come in to greet us with thunderous acclamation. The waves were about 6 to 8 feet in height and wide, impossibly wide. It felt like each wave was encircling the globe, holding the earth together, cleansing and renewing. Their immense power was not threatening, but inviting. Each wave seemed to say "This is how it is, and you are part of it". Without thinking, we burst into song. This was not our custom, but it seemed the only way we could respond to the hospitality of the sea. We sang word for word an ancient hymn of praise *The Gloria*. We did not feel silly or grandiose. It felt right. For on that day, we saw the ocean for the first time.

Now I am not ascribing emotion or cognition to the sea. It is not, as far as I know, a sentient being. There is no mutual apprehension. We cannot project human attributes on to the environment. But I love the sea. Each time I am by the sea, I am a better, saner, more compassionate human being. For others, it will be a mountain range, the desert, a forest or a river or the infinite range of creatures; maybe even a polar bear. The critical thing is that we share connections of all kinds with the environment, which have the capacity to evoke love. It is not the same as love for a person; we know that, and we know the difference between the two experiences of love. But we know that it is love. Once looked at in this way we have a new regard for the world and it is this sense of regard that lies at the heart of the quirky kingdom. We begin to look at the earth, the sky, the sea and all its creatures, from within the horizon of love. We can no longer look at the economic and political issues surrounding the environment the way we did before. The environment is not a distant object or an unlimited resource. It is a gift. Perhaps then the ancient creation myths got this right, in that God entrusted the earth to us as a precious gift and not as a disposable possession.

DOWNSIDE UP

In the West, it seems that society is more tolerant now of homosexuality than previous eras, but thinly veiled suspicion and open contempt for gay and lesbian people are still prevalent. It is hard to know to what extent attitudes have actually changed. In the Church, there is division. In the Anglican Communion there is great division. So, it is clear that we need to address the issues of difference and vulnerability in order to find a way forward, but this is not just a *head* thing. We do not solve it as if it was an academic problem or a moral principle. It is a matter of the *heart*. So I am taking up and extending the invitation of the countercultural Jesus to look with new eyes at lesbian and gay people *as people* from within the horizon of love. But the outcome of this process may not be what we expected, because if love is there, then we will be turned upside down.

People over Principles

In the halcyon days of spin the bottle, we were naïve about matters of love and life. For instance, babies just happened. And most of us tried to convince ourselves that there were no gay or lesbian people in our schools or our families. There was, however, an endearing pair of *spinsters* called Giselle and Maxine, who lived together for years at the end of the street, but they were just good friends. Even if we had our suspicions about family members, they were soon dismissed. With a raised eyebrow, a family member would say "There are reasons why Aunt Dorothy never married" or "Adrian has not met the right girl yet". Of course, even the use of the term *suspicions* implied that there was something wrong or clandestine about gay and lesbian people. Nonetheless, in those innocent days, they were invisible. We could not see them, because we did not want to.

In my 20s, I returned to the Church. There were many reasons for the change. I was mainly drawn by the counter-cultural Jesus. He was no longer the sentimental figure of my childhood who was kind to children, able to walk on water and leap tall buildings in a single bound. I was particularly fascinated by his relationship with the invisible ones of his time. He had compassion for them, which is good, but he also sought them out and enjoyed their company. So, I was keen to explore this new Jesus with kindred spirits. It seemed logical then that I would check out the local parish church. To my surprise, the people I met were gracious and hospitable. But not everyone I met was like that.

About that time I attended a discussion group, on the topic of ethics and Christianity, where I was greeted warmly by a tall, pleasant looking, older man all of 40. In due course, the topic of homosexuality came up and I asked naively, "What is the problem?" To my dismay, the older man bellowed "It's a matter of principle!" He proceeded to hurl biblical hand grenades at me and the other group members, while roundly condemning homosexuality. All the time repeating the catchphrase "It's a matter of principle!" He then quietly got up, left the group and never returned.

The phrase *it's a matter of principle* is a curious one. Invariably it is a handy grab-bag for a bundle of deeply-held feelings and opinions. When we bring out these grab-bags, we rarely bring clarity or wisdom to the conversation. In this mood, it is chiefly a defensive position, the purpose of which is to bolster our own position.

I want to talk about our cultural grab-bag. The key issue is the importance of understanding the principles that form our views on homosexuality; in particular, the taken for granted *matters of principle* that shape our thinking. The influence of these principles remains largely untested. This means that untried principles covertly run the show. Specifically, the unproven principle that homosexuality is wrong exerts undue influence on the debate in the life of Church; such that the debate is neither fair nor open.

In relation to homosexuality, there are three big-ticket items in the Western grab-bag of untested principles. They are *homosexuality is wrong, homosexuality is unnatural* and *procreation is the definitive measure of human sexuality and identity.* These unproven principles are often put forward with the additional support that they are apparently an essential part of the orthodox faith and practice of the Church. This is an example of what I mentioned earlier as the rhetorical use of the term orthodoxy. In practice, the term *orthodoxy* is used in two ways: technical and rhetorical. The technical use of the term *orthodoxy* incorporates views of early church councils, creeds and leading figures. The rhetorical use of the term *orthodoxy* covers many things. In general, the purpose of this usage is to persuade people about the rightness of a particular view. This is achieved at the expense of divergent views that are caricatured and dismissed, implicitly or explicitly, as liberal, progressive, humanist or secular thinking. The rhetorical aim is to inhibit debate by discrediting opposing views and speakers, in order to prevent a fresh examination of untested positions. It is not a loving way to hold a conversation.

Since the 1960s, some academics, politicians and journalists have tried to challenge this kind of thinking, only to be dismissed glibly as being politically correct, even heretical. The battle cry is "Homosexuality is wrong, it's a matter of principle but the liberals just don't get it". So, what is the underlying problem? This *matter of principle* presumes from the outset that homosexuality is wrong. The presumption hinges on the issue of what is natural, because historically what is natural has been regarded as right and proper. This means that homosexuality, which is regarded as unnatural, is wrong by definition. But how do we know what is natural or unnatural? Is the distinction so clear? Who determines this to be the case? What's more, is this the best way of categorizing the complexities of human sexual identity?

I will address these questions in due course, but listing them together here shows something of the collective power of these driving principles. They are formidable. In particular, the natural/unnatural distinction is the Trojan horse of moral controversies. Once you let it in, then it is hard not to be over-run by the thinking that insinuates homosexuality is wrong because it is unnatural. That is, once you accept uncritically the natural/unnatural distinction as the basis for making judgments about sexual identity and human relationships, then there is little chance of looking at issues relating to homosexuality with new eyes. More importantly, it means the focus is on *the problem* of homosexuality rather than the well-being of gay and lesbian *people*.

The key question concerns why homosexuality is considered as unnatural. Let's look at it from two angles: the social context and the issue of procreation. The first aspect concerns the big picture. It goes like this: marriage is an important cultural institution. It is an indispensable building block and as such, it is *the* benchmark for making judgments about relationships and individuals. We learn a lot about the influence of this kind of thinking from pejorative phrases like "She's a *single* mother" or "He's been married *before*". In this light, an intact heterosexual marriage is regarded as inherently right. No explanation required.

This sense of the moral rightness of heterosexual marriage is seen as an integral part of what it means to be a *Christian*. It is the air we breathe. In religious settings, heterosexual marriage is the gold standard, because it is seen as divinely instituted. In the second biblical creation story, for example, the relationship between Adam and Eve becomes the template for all human relations. In contrast, a homosexual partnership is usually not regarded as a valued institution but rather as a deviant practice. By inference, the use of the word *practice* implies that it is not a question of human *relations* but of sexual *activities*. The phrase *deviant practice* expresses the negative judgment that these activities, and those people who participate in them, stray from the norm. In other words, from the outset homosexual partnerships are presumed to be unnatural. No questions asked.

The second aspect concerns the idea of procreation. For the sake of argument, let's presume the validity of the natural/unnatural distinction and ask what it is that makes homosexuality unnatural? The argument goes like this. Heterosexual relations are foundational and marriage is the bedrock of society. Further, heterosexual relations are seen as natural, largely by defining what is natural on the basis of procreation. This is a moral rather than a scientific interpretation of biology, which sets the agenda for what it means to be a proper human being. As a result of this narrow definition, homosexual relations are regarded as unnatural. So, *procreation* is an important item in the Western grab-bag.

The hidden impact of this driving principle has implications for determining what is natural, what is right and what it means to be a proper human being. Specifically, it has a toxic effect on a wide range of people who are divorced, who cannot have children, who have lost children or who have chosen not to have children. This is because the principle of procreation determines what it means to be a proper human being. A proper human being is in a heterosexual relationship that produces children. On the procreation scale, the people I have just mentioned have failed as people. A classic example of this is a recently divorced person, who very quickly learns that he or she has joined the pariah caste, especially in the Church, because they were given the chance to be a proper human being but failed. In my view, double standards, hypocrisy and the inability to forgive are not traits of the quirky kingdom.

And Now the Bible

The argument that homosexuality is wrong as a matter of principle is made on the basis of a number of dubious presumptions. First, homosexuality is judged as wrong because it is unnatural; but the unnatural/natural distinction is suspect. Second, homosexuality is judged as unnatural because of its link with procreation; but the use of the concept of procreation is highly questionable. In all, this *matter of principle* is intellectually weak and destructive. Of course the rejoinder is: what about the Bible?

Many a time I have sat in church synods and councils and listened to fundamentalists in particular refer to the Bible's clear, unambiguous and timeless condemnation of homosexuality. This is often introduced under the banner of *a plain reading* of the Scriptures. The slogan *a plain reading* usually means that a theologically narrow and prescriptive interpretation of a biblical reference is apparently self-evident to people of sound faith. The slogan, however, is more a rhetorical device for short-circuiting debate, than a reliable method for interpreting a complex and ancient book like the Bible.

The Bible, which is an authoritative book for me, can be a difficult work to interpret. For example, the Bible condemns incest, rape and adultery but permits prostitution, polygamy, slavery, sex with slaves and early marriage (for the girl 11-13). When the fundamentalist proponents are questioned about these biblical quandaries, they often parrot more biblical references, but parroting information is not the same as providing sound evidence, a credible explanation, or listening compassionately to gay and lesbian people. So what does the Bible say?

First, there are only six references in the Bible to something akin to homosexuality. These references are open to a wide range of interpretations, especially as there is no word for *homosexual* in Hebrew or Greek, the original languages of the Bible. This alone gives pause for thought. Second, in the ancient world, there is no conception of sexual *orientation*, heterosexual or homosexual. Once more, this cautions us against trying to extract unambiguous modern principles from doubtful ancient texts. This ancient culture also had little understanding of biological and psychological causes. For instance, it attributed mental illness to demonic possession. Third, of the six references, only one appears to be relevant (Romans 1:27). For the author the apostle Paul, however, there are bigger issues at stake than the sexual behavior of heterosexual men (Romans 1:29-31). So, let's not exaggerate the significance of one verse, which is usually taken out of context.

What about the context? In Romans, the sin is that some heterosexual men have turned from the Jewish norm of hetero-sexual relations to same-sex relations. This is regarded by Paul as symptomatic of their failure to render allegiance to God. Significantly, this is the sin of idolatry, which is Paul's *chief* concern. In this instance, heterosexual men have drifted from what is construed as *natural* to the *unnatural*. From an ancient philosophical perspective, this is going against the established order of things. This is compounded by the fact that such a trans-formation involves a heterosexual man adopting a *receptive* position, which is judged negatively, because this is seen as the *female* position. Clearly, the text is not dealing with a modern appreciation of homosexual orientation. On the contrary, it is dealing with an ancient cultic situation where heterosexual men are participating in same-sex relations.

In conclusion, neither the Bible nor the Church's tradition provide clear, succinct and unambiguous explanations condemning homosexuality. In addition, there is no known record of Jesus offering an opinion on homosexuality. In the end, we can only fall back on his emphatic preaching and teaching about the inclusive nature of the quirky kingdom. While there are only a few doubtful biblical references relating to homosexuality, there are many clear biblical references relating to the quirky kingdom of love that was so central to the ministry of Jesus. In fact, the character and generous spirit of the Jesus movement cries out love; an audacious and inclusive love. Homosexuality, nevertheless, is a problem for much of the Church. But why is it a problem? It is the problem of *difference* and the fear of being *unzipped*: figuratively and literally.

What about Love

The idea that homosexuality is indisputably wrong, immoral, unnatural and evil seems to be an integral part of recent thinking. Ironically, it is often presented as a timeless and universal moral law. It is a matter of principle and the inference is that good people know this. As this attitude has been passed from generation to generation, it is hard to look at human identity and sexuality, let alone gay, lesbian, bisexual, transgender or transsexual people, with new eyes. While sections of wider society have been challenging this attitude for some time, the Church is another matter. In particular, the issue has been simmering away in the Anglican Church. It came to a head for me personally in 2004, but before I cut to the heart of matter, let me provide some relevant background information.

In 1998 the Lambeth Conference, an international forum of Anglican bishops, endorsed a resolution relating to human sexuality known as Resolution I.10. It is a curious resolution in the way it holds together uneasily respect for people on the one hand, and matters of principle on the other. In brief, the resolution affirms that God loves gay and lesbian people. It reassures them that "all baptised, believing and faithful persons" are full members of the Church "regardless of sexual orientation". It rejects, however, homosexual practice, the legitimizing or blessing of same-sex unions and the ordination of people who are in same-sex unions. In 2003, the issue came to the boil with the consecration of Gene Robinson as Bishop of New Hampshire in the Episcopal Church of the United States of America. Gene Robinson was openly in a same-sex relationship.

In 2004 I attended General Synod, which is the national forum of the Anglican Church of Australia, in Western Australia. There were a number of agenda items relating to homosexuality. After motions sympathetic to gay and lesbian people had been scuttled, I tried to move a motion without notice, which affirmed that gay and lesbian people were welcome in our parish churches. The motion was neither binding nor enforceable. It was a watchword, the intention of which was to lend moral and spiritual support to *the invisible ones* by openly declaring and affirming our commitment to the hospitality of Jesus. That is, it expressed a sentiment and a value, which was germane to the spirit and heart of the Christian message of love. I admit, however, it was at the end of a very long meeting. Many of us were yawning, fidgeting, doodling and clock-watching, all thinking of the flight back home. But I felt troubled by the conduct of the foregoing debate. There was something dishonest about it. It was very polite, at least superficially, but the restrained intensity of the debate did not match the gravity of the issues. In addition, the *problem* of homosexuality had been discussed in a clinical manner with little or no regard for lesbian and gay *people*. The personal dimensions were presumed to be immaterial.

The president of Synod was sympathetic to the spirit of my motion, so he let me speak. But as I stood up to address the gathering, I was relentlessly jeered by a rowdy minority. It was shocking and I was speechless, but I remember thinking at the time, "What buttons have I pressed here?" While the majority of

Synod members sat in stunned silence and were perhaps sensitive to my cause, I decided to withdraw the motion. Clearly, I had misread the mood of Synod, as I had thought that a positive, welcoming motion would have been universally endorsed. So I trudged back to my seat, trying my best to look composed. As I sat down a synod member from a largely fundamentalist diocese was still yelling at me. He was red-faced, raucous and hateful. Eventually he stopped yelling and turned around to face his equally voluble companion and together they laughed heartily, as if something very funny had happened at Synod. I missed the joke.

There was nothing Christian, let alone human, about Synod that afternoon. It was disgraceful. It was more like the Coliseum than a Christian forum. As a result, the personal dimensions were ignored: that is people did not matter as love had gone. Considering I was a bit player on the Synod stage, the intensity of the reaction was astounding. In retrospect, I do not believe my motion was as ill-conceived or as poorly timed as I had first thought. It proved to be a seismograph, which accurately measured the shifting and grinding of the tectonic plates that lie beneath the Anglican crust. For the first time some of Synod's members were honest. I did not like what they said, but they were transparent. Earlier, they had spoken of important principles and biblical references. They were pretending to be polite, but it all seemed strained. They often began by saying smugly "I have a friend who is homosexual, but..." which was quickly followed by "Of course I love the sinner, but hate the sin". Worse still, they openly smiled as they made serious statements that had grave repercussions for real people. In the end, it was a sad day. No one won. Certainly, lesbian and gay members of Synod and the Australian Church suffered another body blow. Not to mention bisexual, transgender or transsexual people. In the end, what kind of victory was it for the fundamentalist-led vocal minority? I guess from their perspective it was *a matter of principle,* and the principle had been successfully defended. But from the perspective of the unconventional kingdom of God, it was a hollow victory.

Downside Up

To reiterate, the legacy of the natural/unnatural distinction is a phantom, which resides in the back of our minds, all the time insinuating that homosexuality is wrong. It was not that long ago when parents and teachers tried to force left-handed children to write with their right hands, because being left-handed was considered unnatural, even sinister. Is operating a computer, eating ice-cream or using hair product immoral because it is unnatural? In practical terms the natural/unnatural distinction proves little. In personal terms it is divisive and destructive for a range of people who are coldly placed in the unnatural category.

The key is the issue of difference. As Miroslav Volf said "The future of our world will depend on how we deal with identity and difference". Specifically, I am curious about what it is that makes some people so hostile to gay and lesbian people. I suspect there is something about both the real and the imagined differences between homosexual and heterosexual people that frightens many heterosexual men and women, and forces some gay and lesbian people into choosing between remaining invisible or becoming a scapegoat who bears the stigmata of unspoken fear. From the perspective of the love horizon, something is out of kilter here.

Like aliens in a 1950s science fiction movie, the mere mention of homosexuality is enough to cause wide-spread panic in the streets, especially in the Church. Even the weight of anecdotal evidence is compelling proof of this cultural aversion. For a start, recall our school days and the use of gay or lesbian labels as a form of insult or slander. It still happens. In addition, the constant use of gay jokes or put-downs in showers at men's sporting clubs is damning. But worse still is the frightening incidence of violence against lesbian, gay, bisexual and trans-gender people.

There are double standards. Like the argument that says: Okay, there may well be this thing called *homosexual orientation*, but they still have a choice. This is absurd. For instance, I am a person of heterosexual orientation, but this does not mean that I consciously decided, at the age of 12, to become heterosexual after weighing up the pros and cons. It just happened. But worse, there are terrible slurs, ranging from the hysteria surrounding the spurious association of homosexuality and pedophilia to the pernicious description of AIDS as "God's judgment" on the gay community. What kind of a god is this? At best this is a punitive god, at worst this is a despot. This is certainly not the God of Jesus who turned the world upside down in the name of love. This is not the God of love who shines through the life of the quirky kingdom. In fact, the slurs and insinuations are symptoms of deep and lasting prejudices. They are signs of fear; for the aliens have landed, so lock up your sons as well as your daughters.

Sometimes, we refuse to be honest about our real fears. So rather than mention gay and lesbian people, let alone talk with them, we seek refuge in notions like *it's a matter of principle* or *the problem of homosexuality*. While I think the arguments behind these slogans are flawed, the rhetorical use of such slogans trivializes, dismisses and dehumanizes lesbian and gay people. By directing attention toward *principle* and *problem*, we make lesbian and gay *people* invisible. They do not count. And wherever people are made invisible, love has gone.

Such a debate, which focuses on *principle* and *problem* while ignoring *people*, is not a Jesus debate. It is not remotely conducted in the spirit of Jesus of the subversive kingdom. Clearly, we have got our priorities the wrong way round.

Jesus turned the world upside down. In so doing, he brought the downside up. Yes, he saw and sought out the invisible ones.

In the process, they were welcomed and incorporated back into the human community, thus making them whole and visible. They were included because they mattered. What is more, the invisible ones understood the true nature of the vocation of Jesus. Recall the woman who hemorrhaged? Remember the blind man who could really see? Call to mind the marginalized people who recognized the ministry of Jesus? The ministry of Jesus was life-turning and world-shaping because he lived without restraint or excuse under the horizon of love. And if we can't see that, then we have not seen him.

So where does the problem lie? In terms of the subversive kingdom, the Church is going about it the wrong way. In terms of homosexuality, and with the notable of the exception of the Episcopal Church of the United States, conversations in the Church are generally focused on *the problem* of homosexuality. What about the problem of heterosexual majorities? What about *our* tears? When are they named? When are we going to have an honest conversation in the Church about what it means to be human? When will we have the courage to name the elephant in the sitting room, that is, our own vulnerability? As soon as we frame the issue as *the problem* of homosexuality, then we treat lesbian and gay people as objects, rather than as human beings, and they become increasingly disenfranchised. It is supposed to be downside up.

In marked contrast, the culmination of the movement against apartheid involved important moral principles, but the cutting edge of the movement was real engagement with the suffering of black South Africans. Thanks to the voices of Nelson Mandela and Desmond Tutu, people stopped, looked and listened to the invisible ones. Unlike my experience at General Synod in 2004, the ethical and political conversations in South Africa took on a different hue as the plight of real people was fully embraced. All this highlights the problem of religion.

The Lutheran theologian Dietrich Bonhoeffer called for a

"religionless Christianity" and the philosopher Jacques Derrida spoke of "religion without religion". In different ways, these scholars highlighted the problem of religion. In the case of Christianity, the Church needs to function as an institution, at some level, to achieve good things central to the life the quirky kingdom. Common worship, mutual support and works of compassion and justice are good examples of the need for living and working together. But if Christianity has rigid boundaries and inflexible rules, and if boundaries and principles are more important than people, then Christianity as an institution is a problem. In the Jesus tradition, it is downside up. This means that for most of us, if we dare choose to love, then it will be love upside down. Our world will be inverted, so that others may live and thrive in love. In the process, we will learn what it means to love.

The Queer Banquet

If I have learnt anything from the life and teachings of Jesus, it is that homosexuality is not the problem. On the contrary, the Church is the problem, because it is out of kilter with the banquet of the quirky kingdom. What's more, I do not mean just the Anglican Church, but the universal Church. In contrast, the gift of gay and lesbian people is that they call all us to account. In this light, it is not gay, lesbian, bisexual, transgender or transsexual people, but the Church which is on trial and the decisive measure of the Church is the measure of love.

Incidentally, I cannot remember bisexual or transgender persons ever being mentioned in an Australian synod. In many ways, they are more *invisible* than gay and lesbian people in the life of the Church. But the presence of bisexual, transgender, transsexual or pansexual persons underlines the futility and destructiveness of limiting human sexuality to two categories: heterosexual or homosexual. As if the diversity and wonder of humanity can be squeezed into two categories. As if the sheer mystery of humanity can be placed methodically on an ecclesiastical spreadsheet. Certainly, the acronym LGBT, which stands for lesbian, gay, bisexual and transgender people, represents a major advance. It transcends the old bifurcation of homosexual and heterosexual that excluded many people from full participation in community by failing to do justice to the staggering complexity of humankind. The development and imposition of this bifurcation not only represents a lack of love, but it is also punitive.

The critical question then is: how does the Church measure up in relation to love? In the Jesus tradition, the banquet is the central metaphor of the subversive reign of God. The banquet is a love feast, open to all. It embodies the essence of Christianity's insight into love. This love is magnanimous and inclusive. It is practical. It is not empty piety, but a passionate work that challenges the status quo, including the status quo of the Church. In this light, the banquet of the kingdom is a quirky banquet, maybe even a queer banquet that is grounded in love.

In my continual returning to Christianity, I understand more and more about the importance of the kingdom. It is the heart of the vision of Jesus: wisdom teacher, prophet and holy one of God. To recapitulate, the kingdom of God is dynamic. It impacts on the present and draws us into the future. As such, it is a subversive presence in the world. It turns things upside down. In fact, it turns things up the right way. It is a rude awakening to the realities and the possibilities of life. So in the name of love, the quirky kingdom names, destabilizes and disrupts unjust customs, structures and institutions. It is iconoclastic, unmasking idolatries, false allegiances and the ubiquitous love-substitutes. Intolerant of intolerance, the quirky kingdom gives short shrift to the tyrants, bullies and abusers of the world, while offering life, creating community and giving love. But here is the tricky part. Typically, the outcome of the presence of the kingdom of God is not what we expect.

At this juncture, and in the spirit of the quirky kingdom, it would be easy for me to wax lyrical about how we should love gay and lesbian people. Of course we should. From a Christian perspective and in the horizon of love: that's a given. The pressing issue is really a question of compassion and justice. How come lesbian, gay, bisexual and transgender people are excluded by the Church *at large* from the unconditional love of God, which we see so clearly in the Jesus stories? But that is not the half of it. It also misses something of the power of the quirky kingdom. When the kingdom is present it is active, it makes things happen and it changes peoples' lives; but the outcome is not what we expect. In other words, if the Church of Jesus is to be compassionate and just, then our world will be turned upside down. It is not simply a matter of us caring for those *on the edge*. We all have to change.

I mentioned earlier that the Church is the problem, not homosexuality. I also argued that lesbian and gay people, because of who they are and their personal experiences, have a substantial contribution to make to the Church, personally and collectively. In addition to the emotional and physical abuse gay and lesbian people endure in society, they have been denied the opportunity to fulfill a calling to ordained ministry, or the ministry of a bishop, as well the opportunity to receive the Church's blessing on their relationships. Clearly, lesbian and gay people of faith have paid double the price. Note also, I refer to *the Church's blessing* as I think God has blessed them already, in spite of the graceless intransigence of the Church. On this basis, I would argue that they have a remarkable insight into the experience of alienation and estrangement, which gives them a unique insight into the heart of the quirky kingdom. Like the marginal ones in the New Testament, they can see. Let's go further.

In the Christian tradition, the *stigmata* refer specifically to the wounds Christ endured on the cross. In a more general way, it can also refer to the marks; that is, *the cost* of following Christ (Galatians 6:17). We should not underestimate the emotional and spiritual cost that gay and lesbian people have paid for being gay or lesbian Christians. The lesbian and gay people who choose to belong to the Church, usually because they have a vision of the quirky kingdom, pay an enormous price for faithfulness. They bear the marks of Christ. They bear the *stigmata*.

On the basis of this experience, lesbian and gay people can lead us to a renewed interest in, and experience of, the life and teachings of Jesus. This is important because the theme of the reign of God in the life of the Church is far too familiar. It has been tamed. We have domesticated the unconventional experience of the kingdom by turning it into a respectable principle and elevating it above the needs and hopes of real people. Let's cast our minds back and recall that the proclamation of the kingdom was troubling. Jesus himself caused offense (the scribes were furious). The presence of the kingdom *is* disturbing. While non-violent, it is inherently subversive and that is why the Romans crucified him. By seeing, listening to and understanding lesbian and gay people, our sisters and brothers, we will rediscover something of the wildness of the kingdom, because the quirky kingdom is primarily queer. The term *queer* is a true and telling description of a countercultural kingdom that is fit for the vicissitudes of the 21st century. By making this link between the term *queer* and the nature of the banquet, I am not intending to hi-jack the term from gay and lesbian thinkers and writers. On the contrary, I want to acknowledge and celebrate the fact that the idea of a queer banquet is a magnanimous gift to all Christians. Certainly, the quirky banquet could also be described as a *rainbow* banquet, which is a bright, inclusive and positive reading of the quirky kingdom. But I have deliberately chosen the term *queer* because it historically has had a negative nuance. This reminds us that Jesus and the quirky kingdom caused offense. Yes, this is love that turns the world up the right way.

I have learnt much from Jesus, Mary Magdalene and the extraordinary movement that discerned and proclaimed the power of the kingdom. In this light, the queer banquet is good news. It makes sense. It brings life. And it begins and ends in love. As we love, as we take others seriously, as we look and understand, others will evoke wonder, love and new wisdom from within us. They will help us see. I suspect that gay and lesbian, transgender and bisexual people presently understand the nature of the kingdom better than the wisdom of all the heterosexuals combined. This is because when you are in the in-group, you cannot always see. Remember: the disciples could not see, but outsiders could. Ironically, while the dream of the queer banquet is a blessing, there is a strong prophetic element too. Unless the Church embodies and enacts the ethos and spirit of the queer banquet, then we have failed our brother Jesus, his friends from Galilee and our marginalized sisters and brothers. In this context, the notion of *the queer banquet* is a measure of the Church's integrity.

Lastly, the idea of blessing is important. The word *blessing*, however, sounds old fashioned and it can certainly be used in a superficial or sanctimonious manner. But in the ancient world a blessing is a powerful thing, because it involves the passing on, through word and gesture, something of the vitality and the life of God. In fact, the significance of this sacred *word and gesture* comes alive in a real community. That is, the blessing is powerful because the faith community sees it as powerful. This is not *hocus pocus*. It is about how hope, trust and expectation, create an atmosphere surcharged with the promise and possibility of the new. In the 21st century, the blessing of same-sex unions and the ordination of practicing gay and lesbian people are sacramental opportunities for the fulfillment of the vision of Jesus for our common life in the quirky kingdom. In the process, the Church is blessed as well as those people who present themselves in faith for the blessing of the Church.

A CELEBRATION OF LOVE

I am celebrating the theme of love, which is the decisive measure of all things Christian. But love is not for the fainthearted as it changes who we are and the world we live in. This is love upside down.

One of its key characteristics concerns the way we see others, because love begins when we look at others as wonderful, irreplaceable people. We see people differently. In reality, when we begin to see others, we see them for the first time. Once we see people this way, watch out, because this will irrevocably change us. Once we look at others through the eyes of love, there is no going back. We would not dream of it.

This love is courageous, big-hearted and inclusive. This means that we gladly accept people as they are, as there is a new generosity of spirit within us that wants the best for them. Simultaneously, they bring out the best in us.

The cutting edge for the horizon of love comes from re-visiting Christianity. Jesus, no longer meek and mild, is a counter-cultural prophet of justice and teacher of love. In his teachings, Jesus concentrates in word and deed on the subversive reign of God. It is a disruptive kingdom; turning the world up the right way.

More than Enough

In the mid 1970s, I spent a month living and working with a group of Maoris; the indigenous people of New Zealand. It was, without exaggeration, a fantastic experience of community. What's more, I suspect my understanding of a faith-community has been permanently shaped more by this experience, than all my study and earnest theological discussions with equally earnest colleagues. My most precious memory is working with Maori people on a hangi. A hangi is a Maori feast, where plentiful amounts of meat and vegetables are steam-cooked all day, in a pit, on heated stones. The fire and the food take hours to prepare. The task of preparation is a community experience in itself. Literally scores of people can be involved in the preparation of a hangi. In the end, it is the feast that counts and this is a feast that welcomes all comers, where food is generously given and there is more than enough. It is a love feast.

The hangi captures the ethos and the spirit of love of the quirky kingdom, which is an extravagant, unconditional, indiscriminate love feast. It is not something we measure and classify. We enjoy, simply enjoy. We enjoy it with others, who bring this love to life. This is the love that Jesus knew. As a result, the critics, scoffers, cynics and naysayers of all persuasions, killed him for it. So forget about a wrathful god; it is human intolerance of love that is dangerous and destructive.

Can you imagine my excitement then when as a young man, I returned to the Church to encounter the countercultural Jesus with his compelling proclamation? Like the hangi, this was indeed a generous feast. There was more than enough and at last, I was being fed. It was not exactly what I expected. For it was touching something within me, a yearning and a whim for a deeper life. I had thought that I was drawn largely by intellectual questions, by my search for meaning, and this is true. But what I discovered was also about heart; the heart to live courageously and to belong with others who dared to love.

Around this time, I read the story of the prodigal or lost son. Be assured this is not sermon time, but the story is a telling vignette of what I gleaned about love from Christianity. Here is the rub of the story: a rich man has two sons. The younger son, the goodtime boy, takes off with his share of the inheritance. He parties on and squanders everything. He experiences suffering, shame and *affliction*. He comes to his senses and returns home expecting to be punished; no longer fit to be called a son. His Father, who is waiting for him, embraces him and celebrates his return. Now the younger son is someone. He has been welcomed. He is loved. He is visible. The Father's response was unexpected. It did not follow the old rules, but rather expressed a new ethos. But note the ending: while the older son, who remained at home, could see all before him, he did not understand.

Christianity's take on experience is part of its wisdom on love. In high-flown terms, this is has links with the theology of the Incarnation, which is about God-in-the-world. So ostensibly the Incarnation refers to the ancient story of the birth of Jesus, but ultimately it expresses something of the nature of the relationship between the divine and human experience. The word *experience* is a tricky customer. It is part and parcel of how we describe our world, our relationships and ourselves. But the word is hard to define. In the past, a certain kind of experience dominated Western culture: abstract, male, individual and heroic. We now speak of a multitude of experiences of equal value. But I do not want to enter this academic minefield. The point is that the idea of experience is an important part of our self-understanding and love is an integral part of experience.

What I discovered on my returning to Christianity is that the radical Jesus speaks directly to our experience. Specifically, Jesus talks about the subversive kingdom of God, and the essence of the life of the quirky kingdom is a dynamic movement from no one to someone, from exclusion to inclusion, from isolation to community. In keeping with the countercultural kingdom: it is upside down and down side up.

In this vision, God's gaze makes us visible. But let me

reiterate: this is not an old man in the sky pushing buttons, causing earthquakes and saving stray dogs. Expel the image of the old man in the sky and recall earthly memories of love. Here we find the divine infusing and enlivening experience.

Within the horizon of love, people are not problems to be solved or categories to be sorted. In fact, all our principles and categories are transcended by love. While principles and categories are transient, love endures. So, in the horizon of love, people are not problems but gifts. This love is a source of sublime wonder expressed as surprise as in "Who is this person?" The wonder has to do with the discovery of the other as irreplaceable. This reminds us too that we cannot absorb, possess or tame another. We may know them well, but they are different. They are a separate other. We accept and delight in the fact that they are *other* and not the same as us. So there is union and separation (*eros* and *agape*). Such love, such mutual respect, enlarges and enriches our vision. It informs and shapes our spirit. It gives heart and voice.

Embracing Difference

It is important that this love is grounded in the real world. One of the biggest problems in the world is that people are different. Differences matter. Certainly, there are some differences that are trivial. But there are significant differences. Some are obvious, others are subtle. Race is a big one. These days, few dinner parties end in an argument over the contribution of Greek immigrants to Australian culture, but there have been such disputes over indigenous Australians. It is a painful example that difference matters and some differences matter a great deal. Remember women have been regarded as *inferior*, the environment as *hostile*, and lesbian and gay people as *deviant*. So, it takes a courageous kind of love to embrace difference, and live with vulnerability. This is love upside down.

Love will not colonize, isolate or annihilate people on the

basis of difference. It respects, honors and embraces difference by inviting us to focus *on people*. The irony of love is that our lives are enriched by concentrating on and attending to others. We become whole-people in relationships that delight in a certain kind of connection, a certain kind of space, where our shared humanity, in all its complexity, is a joy. This happens when the other person ceases to be a useful object or an annoying obstacle and becomes the incomparable other in whom we delight. This sense of delight has two aspects, in that we take comfort in our similarities and we gain inspiration from our differences. The differences are no longer seen as threatening but as emanating from their sheer otherness. The sense of their strangeness, or the otherness of others, makes them who they are. It makes them interesting and awe-inspiring. And it all gets down to the idea and the experience of love.

Love rings true. Love makes us feel. It makes us weep and laugh. It affects our attitudes and behavior. Love, also, has a big say in how we interpret the meaning of our lives. Understandably, the question of meaning is a modern problem and everyone has tried to put their spin on it, from rock stars to talk show hosts. Meaning is important, but it is hard to define. By meaning, I am not falling back on a rarefied academic theory. By meaning, I am not referring to pop-culture's easy wisdom and the positive-thinking industry, which has tapped into the search for meaning, often setting up people for disappointment. What happens if you do not become a movie star, prime minister or the president? No, meaning finds its home in relationships, in love and in the celebration of difference.

Of course, the Jesus tradition has something to say about meaning. But what about the Church that is supposed to embody the Jesus movement? Let's be real. Let's remember human nature. Let's recall the football pie night and Bruce who ate all the sausage rolls. At bottom, there is something troubling about human nature, in particular, power and institutions.

Nonetheless, while the Church has its share of fruitcakes, hypocrites and tyrants, the majority of the laity, the people in the pews as well as bishops, priests and ministers are decent and compassionate people. What's more the Church, including its tradition, has many good things to say about how *meaning* is found and fostered in our shared experience of love. The big problem is structure. This refers to the human proclivity toward hierarchies, which privilege a few at the expense of the many. The structure breeds, and harbors, villains and despots, especially when we remain silent. While many churches are more vigilant in this regard, in terms of accountability and transparency, there is always a danger that, if oppressive structures are not changed, then innocent people will suffer.

So what is this structure? Structure is about how we fit, work and live together. It is about enduring social processes or patterns that enable or inhibit shared life. While this would seem an obvious criticism of the explicitly hierarchical Anglican, Catholic and Orthodox churches, it is also true of many congregational-protestant churches. Many of the latter officially claim to be democratically organized, community-based institutions, but implicitly they often cultivate destructive hierarchies. For example, the tendency to hierarchy in some protestant churches can be found where the pastor is feted as *the* bible teacher, who has exclusive authority to render a plain reading of Scripture for *his* flock. In other words, he determines *the truth*. Institutions, however, of all persuasions can get in the way of love; especially in the Church where principles or biblical texts, rituals or symbols, run the risk of becoming objects of worship. So, what is the way forward?

Love, One More Time
In terms of the Church, as an institution, the key is found in maintaining flexible or porous boundaries, and not allowing them to become rigid or impervious. The test of the health of

these boundaries is how we cope with difference. Who is in and who is out. Who is welcome and who is not. Who is visible and who is invisible. For centuries, many good clergy and countless laity have kept the boundaries fuzzy and flexible. When the boundaries became fixed, they quietly rebelled in the name of love. They were willing to be vulnerable and to have their worlds turned upside down by love. The problem though with flexible and porous boundaries is that they are not neat and tidy. It messes with the Church, although this is a good thing.

Institutions are unavoidable. For example, once a book club decides it needs to put in writing how it works, and starts appointing people to official positions; it is in the process of creating an informal association that has the potential of becoming an institution. But it is not a bad thing. As social animals we need to establish shared values, common purposes and mutually beneficial practices. We need to determine and allocate roles and responsibilities. In the case of the Church, the problem occurs when the structure of the institution becomes its raison d'être. So what will keep the Church alive, supple, open and courageous? The health and the relevance of the Church, as an institution, is related to the capacity of its leaders and its people to re-visit, re-discover and re-claim the love espoused by Jesus of the quirky, queer, unconventional and subversive reign of God. This is love upside down. And this love will mess with the Church, because people are more important than principles.

Over the centuries, the Church has become more institutionalized and less personal. In retrospect, the worst thing that happened to the Church was the Emperor Constantine's successful take-over bid in the fourth century. Since then, we have invented new names for *matters of principles* and the number of rules has proliferated as edicts, canons and ordinances have multiplied. Some of the rules were helpful for our life together, but many others killed the spirit, as we lost sight of the intrinsic value, the sheer delight and sublime wonder, of people. We have had great leaders, but too often we have entrusted the privilege of leadership to bullies, who like boys at a pie night, wanted to eat all the sausage rolls. Worse still, we let them stay there, because we rashly believed it was the will of God.

Since the 1950s, and with the possible exception of the United States, the Church has become increasingly marginalized in the West. For many Christians, there is a sense of grief about the loss of place and voice. Ironically, the general interest in spirituality seems to rising. I see this as an important opportunity for a global conversation about love; and God knows the world needs it. Unfortunately, the Anglican Church has been preoccupied of late with the unity of the Anglican Communion. Maybe we are heading toward a permanent split? It is hard to say. But before we get to that point, I would like us to try love, one more time.

While the Anglican Church does not own love, there is wonderful, feisty and creative tradition of love within Anglicanism that has its roots in Celtic Christianity and the medieval mystics. Indeed, the best of Anglicanism is a quirky comprehensiveness that holds together in tension, in love, a rainbow-like array of opinions, people and cultures. From the outside, we have probably looked a very muddled institution at times, but historically that messiness has expressed a passionate commitment to the subversive Jesus, who holds together all things in love. I am not for a moment thinking there is an easy answer, but I am convinced love is our only hope. Love, the love of people, the upside down love of the disruptive kingdom, changes us, our conversations and their outcomes. It is never too late for love. Even if we must go our separate ways, and that would be regrettable, let's do it in love.

But do we dare trust love again? In reality, millions of people of all persuasions keep returning to love. They know intuitively that love is the only thing that matters. Continually good people allow themselves to be swept up by the vision and the experience of love. They have had the freedom, wisdom and grace to love deeply and live boldly. Certainly there have been a few crackpots, but the majority of ordinary Christians are committed to love. By ordinary Christians, I am also including good bishops, priests, ministers and above all else, the laity. The laity is the Church's term for pew-sitters, fans in the bleachers or punters at the rail. God bless them all; they do most of the work. My experience is that these people have survived and thrived because of love. Over the centuries, innumerable Christians and Christian communities have faithfully rebelled against the structures, the legalism and the tyrants, quietly and with perseverance, openly and with vigor, all in the name of love.

The Church's pathological tendency toward a blind adherence to principles over people betrays a poverty of spirit. I suspect this harsh legalism is at best a love-substitute and at worst a form of social control. Naturally, I am not talking about practical-concrete things, like repairing the downpipe on the church hall. If I was building a house, in consultation with an architect, I would expect the builder to follow the plan. When it comes to relationships, and to the ethical quandaries of human existence, there is no infallible plan. I suspect a lack of a plan drives some people crazy; at the least, it causes great anxiety. Sadly, if there is not an ardent commitment to love and a genuine appreciation of others as a source of wonder, then a punitive legalism fills the void. All this is part of the problem of difference.

It all gets back to vulnerability, the elephant in the sitting room, and how difference can make us feel vulnerable. This is because difference mucks up our plans. It unzips us and puts us in a position where we must make a choice. Either we ignore differences, insist on principles and live with the appearance of certainty or we engage with people, insist on love and live with the reality of vulnerability. This is easily said, but hard to do.

Only a wonderful, passionate and subversive experience of love will enable us to rise above the paralyzing effects of our many fears, known and unknown. This is part and parcel of life and of what it means to be a human being. So I am not throwing out all the rules, but making a plea in the name of love, and the memory of Jesus, to focus on people first. While it will never be as neat as this, the intention to love and to engage can keep us alive and make us whole.

In the Name of Love

I can see with clarity, the moment I fell in love with Sally. I remember clutching the bottle, not knowing what was to come. With heedless enthusiasm, I twisted the daylights out of the bottle, which fortuitously pointed toward Sally. It was a small death, but it was also a moment of transfiguration. For when I looked at Sally, she was looking at me with that gaze of tender recognition, quietly taking me in. I was no longer the amusing but sometimes annoying boy, who sat at the back of the classroom. At long last I had been seen, and I could see. On that night, I saw Sally for the first time. It was love at first sight. The combination of being unzipped and Sally's unsolicited gift was inconceivable. I cannot tell you what was in her mind, let alone her heart, but she looked.

The older I get, the less I know, and the less it matters. The only thing that matters is love. As I look back on my life, it is the exquisite, serendipitous and disturbing moments of love that have given me the elation of grace and the consolation of dignity. More than this, experiences of love have given me courage in the face of fear and uncertainty. This is because love puts everything in perspective; it forms a new horizon, which enables me to say "This doesn't matter" or "This matters and I will risk every-thing". All this, however, is far more than a distillation of my personal experience. It has a lot to do with my experience of revisiting Christianity, throwing out the baggage and encoun-tering the subversive Jesus. In spite of the failings of the insti-tution; countless Christians and Christian communities have lived with courage under the horizon of love. In keeping with the

Jesus tradition, the invisible have been seen, heard and welcomed. This is love upside down.

While love does not solve all our problems, it changes the way we see people and the way we respond to them. In particular, it invites us to respond to people first, such that we see them differently, we act differently and we are transformed in the process of this awakening. The injection of a Christian perspective on love enriches and expands the love horizon. It provides it with new content and impetus. Such that, with love as the horizon, we have a framework that makes sense of life, because it has the capacity to provide new bearings, as it incorporates the wisdom of the subversive Jesus. This enables us to do the work of love.

So I am celebrating love; the courageous and compassionate love of the quirky kingdom. This is no love-substitute; this is the real thing. This is also the love of ordinary, yet daring people, who choose to live with vulnerability as they embrace those who are different. This love invites us to take others seriously, so that people become more important than matters of principle, biblical texts or religious dogma. We see them for the first time. It may not happen right away, but there is a shift from disinterest to engagement, from carefully calculating to joyously participating, while experiencing love all the more.

Love as horizon does not mean human existence is easy or that we easily solve complex ethical dilemmas. It changes, however, the way we address life and its problems. In particular, because we live in the presence of the unconventional kingdom, we have a deep emotional and spiritual commitment to living the way of love.

The love of the quirky kingdom finds its ultimate expression in community, where love gives form and content to faith communities. This is a community of relations in which there is an intimate connection between its members; where individuals experience each other as sacred. This is the key; this is the divine glue which holds all things together: the other person is a gift.

And this is cause for celebration.

Love is complex. It is subject to change but capable of longevity, through thick and thin, success and failure, triumph and tragedy. It is redeeming, even transcendent. It has many aspects working as one: the experience of deep intimacy and sublime delights; of being filled and emptied, of holding on and letting go.

We know how sweet this love can be, because we have tasted the bitterness of its absence. Because we were lost, we know the joy of being found. Because we were no one, we know the power of being someone. Because we have been seen, we see and understand. Such love rings true for us, because it is an expression of our deepest and most authentic aspirations. It inspires us to take another risk, build community, engage the world and seek justice with compassion.

Chapter

FURTHER READING

Bonhoeffer, D. *Letters and Papers from Prison: Dietrich Bonhoeffer Works* (Philadelphia: Fortress Press, 2010).

Caputo, J.D. ed. *Deconstruction in a Nutshell: A Conversation with Jacques Derrida* (New York: Fordham University Press, 1997); while there are hidden gems in Derrida, reading it is hard work; so this is an excellent introduction to his work, especially on issues like *difference* and the problems of *community*.

Farley, M.A. *Just Love: A Framework for Christian Sexual Ethics* (New York and London: Continuum, 2006); a clear, thoughtful and comprehensive presentation on sexual ethics, with a useful examination of the relevant biblical references.

Gadamer, H. *Truth and Method* (London and New York: Continuum, 1975, 1989, 2004); a heavy-duty book with great ideas like the concept of horizon.

Gaita, R. *Good and Evil: An Absolute Conception* (London and New York, Routledge, 1991, 2004); a great work, which is a demanding read, but rewarding because it is well written.

Heyward, C. *Touching Our Strength: The Erotic as Power and the Love of God* (Harper Collins: San Francisco, 1989); a modern classic, partly because of the courage she displays in addressing the issues.

Lambeth Conference Official Website for details on Resolution I.10.

Nussbaum, M.C. *Upheavals of Thought: The Intelligence of Emotions* (New York: Cambridge University Press, 2001, 2003); a heavy-duty work with insights on love and the emotions.

Reid, D. ed. *John Gaden: A Vision of Wholeness* (Alexandria, NSW: E.J. Dwyer, 1994); a wonderful collection of essays by a gifted scholar and a devoted priest.

Schussler Fiorenza, E. *Jesus: Miriam's Child, Sophia's Prophet: Critical Issues in Feminist Christology* (New York: Continuum,

1994); a terrific introduction to an appreciation of the subversive Jesus and his friends from Galilee.

Singer, I. *Philosophy of Love: A Partial Summing-Up* (Cambridge, Massachusetts; London, England: The MIT Press, 2009); a short, interesting and readable philosophical survey on love.

Springsted, E.O. ed. *Simone Weil* (Maryknoll, New York: Orbis Books, 1998).

Volf, M. *Exclusion and Embrace: A Theological Exploration of Identity, Otherness, and Reconciliation* (Nashville: Abingdon Press, 1996); a theological exploration of the impact of difference.

OTHER BOOKS BY STEVEN OGDEN

I Met God in Bermuda: Faith in the 21ˢᵗ Century (Winchester, UK; Washington, USA: O-Books, 2009) ISBN 978-1-84694-204-4. Endorsements:

"Can anything new be said about religion, the oldest human obsession? Probably not, but in this compelling book Steven Ogden has at least found a new way of talking about it". Richard Holloway; former Anglican Primus of Scotland.

"*I Met God in Bermuda* is a quirky, thoughtful and compassionate demonstration that the essence of faith is doubt and that, to mean anything at all, faith must be integrated with our knowledge and experience of the world we live in". Hugh Mackay; social researcher, author.

"Steven Ogden has written a 21st Century *Honest to God* and he has done it with wit and wisdom. He gives his readers an engaging and lively postmodern riposte to the new atheists and cultural despisers of Christianity today." Michael Northcott, Professor of Ethics University of Edinburgh

"Ogden outlines a true 'faith seeking understanding'... which acknowledges the metaphorical nature of theological discourse. This is a challenging but essential introduction to Christian faith in our contemporary world". Stephen Platten; Bishop of Wakefield, Chair of the Church of England's Liturgical Commission

"How can we reconcile suffering with a God of love? Steven Ogden tackles this crucial question with a rare combination of exemplary, honest theological engagement and a lively energizing prose style. *I Met God in Bermuda* is immediately accessible for a wide audience, making this a book that should be on every parish's study schedule". Dr Muriel Porter; historian, author, journalist.

"This welcome book... is based both on personal spiritual

experience and on a broad theological knowledge and expertise. Steven Ogden is a good and honest communicator of complex issues to a generation often confused by the spiritual marketplace as well as by various extreme expressions of religion". Andrew R St John, Bishop and Rector, Church of the Transfiguration, New York

NEXT BOOK

Steven's next book develops a contemporary theology of humanity by exploring ugliness and beauty. This will not be a dry study of aesthetics, but an open and forthright account of how we determine what is ugly or beautiful in the first place, the practical implications of being labeled accordingly, and the relationship between ugliness, beauty and spirituality.

CONTACT DETAILS

Website: www.stevenogden.com
Email: stevengogden@gmail.com

B O O K S

O is a symbol of the world, of oneness and unity. In different cultures it also means the "eye," symbolizing knowledge and insight. We aim to publish books that are accessible, constructive and that challenge accepted opinion, both that of academia and the "moral majority."

Our books are available in all good English language bookstores worldwide. If you don't see the book on the shelves ask the bookstore to order it for you, quoting the ISBN number and title. Alternatively you can order online (all major online retail sites carry our titles) or contact the distributor in the relevant country, listed on the copyright page.

See our website **www.o-books.net** for a full list of over 500 titles, growing by 100 a year.

And tune in to myspiritradio.com for our book review radio show, hosted by June-Elleni Laine, where you can listen to the authors discussing their books.

MySpiritRadio